CACOPHONY TO SYMPHONY

Evincepub Publishing

Parijat Extension, Bilaspur, Chhattisgarh 495001

First Published by Evincepub Publishing 2020

Copyright © Ankit Khemka 2020

All Rights Reserved.

ISBN: 978-93-90197-14-9

Price: Rs.599/-

CACOPHONY

TO

SYMPHONY

Proven guide to transform your software product
development from chaos to order

ANKIT KHEMKA

Om Ganeshay Namah!

Writing the book was tough, concluding it was terrific!

Thank you, God Almighty, for providing me the chance to express my learnings, and perseverance to share it in this book.

My immense gratitude and heartfelt thanks to -

- My parents for their blessings, my wife and son for their unconditional love and patience.
- My teachers for imparting knowledge and showing us the right direction. I miss you, Radhika mam. RIP!
- My friends and partners in crime, this would not have been possible without you
- My teams and colleagues, for being my strength and the reason for my enthusiasm to work every day. I love you all!
- My mentors and managers, for believing in me and providing opportunities and guidance throughout
- Evincepub for designing, marketing and publishing my book

Contents

About the Author

Ankit is a motivated, personable technology & management professional with more than 15 years' experience in software product development and services space. He has led multi-million transformational programs internationally for some of the marquee organizations in product development, banking, finance, and oil exploration domain. He comes with tremendous experience in executing and completing wide-ranging programs, blended with business and technology of all sizes and challenges. Over the years, he has engaged and worked closely with the customers, solving their problems by playing diverse roles - developer, technology lead, project manager, market researcher, engineering manager, program and account owner.

Ankit graduated with a Bachelor of Engineering degree in Computer Science from V.J.T.I, Mumbai. Further, he completed globally-recognized executive programs in business analytics, sales, and marketing. Ankit has the knack for numbers and love for data visualization.

When he is not working, Ankit is probably hanging out with his friends, traveling, or building cool LEGO structures with his son.

———•———

Cacophony To Symphony

Praise for 'Cacophony To Symphony'

The present time is where there has been a quick and remarkable improvement in technology. As a result, the technology users have become more evolved and aware of the changes in technology and demand better and better every day. This has led to the companies, and organizations in this field to become more competitive and work with more zeal and resilience to provide the best of the best to the consumers. But amidst all this, there are flaws and problems which Ankit Khemka talks about in his book, "Cacophony to Symphony: Proven Guide to Transform Your Software Product Development from Chaos to Order".

The author makes an interesting play of words in choosing the title which does not give the slightest clue or idea about what the book is going to talk about. But the subtitle gives a fair idea of the book being a guide to better software product development and making sure that everything remains fine and intact throughout the process.

The author gives a preface and an introduction to the book where he explains his idea of writing the book and the circumstances which made him resort to his pen. He clearly states that he intends to keep the book as a guide to readers to help the fellow people in his field and guide them through based on his experience and learning over the years.

Ankit begins "Cacophony to Symphony" by an introduction wherein he presents a properly analyzed data in front of the readers. This presentation of data adds weight to the venture that he is to take up in the coming pages. Thereafter, he goes to the root of the problem in a scientific manner. He makes the readers inquisitive by asking them a series of questions in between the text which also makes them wonder and question things while answering him at the same time. Thereafter, he begins to enrich the knowledge of the reader regarding how cacophony can be avoided and how things can be run smoothly. He gives various ideas to understand the dynamics in the current scenario, what is it that the customers really want, time to time brainstorming sessions, decision-making, and the things to keep in mind when deciding, and last but not the least, the importance of communication. In this manner, the author covers a variety of aspects and trying his best to cater to whatever needs may come in the working of anyone.

Experience gives birth to wisdom, and the author exercises his wisdom in "Cacophony to Symphony" to explain his ideas based on the probable situations and circumstances he could think of. The creation of such situations and incorporating them into the space of the book makes "Cacophony to Symphony" more of a practical experience for the readers instead of being a mere theoretical set of thoughts and ideas. Even by reading, the readers can understand situations like they are being explained to them in person and sometimes it sounds like attending a class, and learning things from a teacher. At times, he takes up explaining things in a step by step form in "Cacophony to Symphony" so when the readers begin to apply the techniques and ideas, it becomes easier for them to remember.

Ankit keeps the content focused and to the point. He talks about the question he raises without beating about the bush. The focused nature of "Cacophony to Symphony" also gives a clue to the clarity of thoughts in the mind of the author. At the same time, he also explains his matters in a concrete form which makes it convenient for the readers to understand things.

The author opts for an easy and fine written language to make sure the book becomes a friendly and comfortable read and language does not become a barrier in restricting anyone's learning through this guide. He also keeps the address in the first person directly to the reader which makes sure that the reader gets involved on a personal level. It also makes sure that the reader begins to respond to the situations created by Ankit and also responds to the questions he raises here and there in "Cacophony to Symphony".

All the readers who are involved in the field of software development and the students of the same subject should definitely read "Cacophony to Symphony" for a better understanding of the ideas. Since the book is a first-person account from a person who has been in the field for a good time and has paid attention to understand the intricacies, and technicalities involved as the years have rolled by, this book becomes a treasure to be kept for learning, and a guide who would be there for help and support from time to time.

**- An extract from the review published at
The Literature Today**
Reviewed By: Akhila Saroha

Cacophony To Symphony

Introduction

Research has shown that 72% of new software products and services innovation fails to deliver on expectations. It implies 7 out of 10 products are outright rejected by the customers as soon as they are launched. Failure to understand customer needs and fixing a non-existent problem are the primary reasons for these products and services to fail.

The primary cause of the collapse could be a dearth of customer focus and rigor during the product development and engineering journey. There are various other internal dynamics within the company and the engineering unit for the downfall of the product. It could be distorted vision & goals, misaligned stakeholders, inadequate demarcation of roles and responsibilities, incoherent engineering processes, lack of discipline, compromising view towards quality, and incompetency in timely decision-making. It leads to wastage of everyone's time in unplanned, random tasks without any unified goal for the team, perpetually resulting in defective software product versions in the market, and substandard customer experience.

Cacophony to Symphony is a step by step guide to transform the software product development shop from chaos to order, from discord to harmony. It walks you through the proven techniques to build software in a much simplified and efficient manner by mitigating, maneuvering through the uncertainties and complexities of the software ecosystem.

The book plunges in the crucial facets of software engineering voyage, that are typically overlooked in a rush to create and deliver products faster. It serves a single point of reference for anyone who plans to venture in a start-up or set up a product development garage from scratch. It is also useful for the small and medium-sized product companies aspiring to shift gears and grow exponentially with better market relevance and sustenance. The book offers you with the fundamental blocks along with its right placement to build a seamless product manufacturing system through standardized processes, best practices with customer-centricity.

Chapter 1

Cacophony and chaos in a product development shop

Software development is not the same as it was 20 or 25 years ago.

The software development landscape is continually changing, and there is a regular paradigm shift in the way market and business operations. Change is the new normal. Customers' demand and expectation have gone up, the competition is getting tighter, and there is an ask to do more with fewer resources. The market is more unpredictable than before, the technology is changing rapidly, and the adoption of the technology is growing at a mind-boggling rate. Today, infants and kids learn to hold a mobile phone faster than their milk bottles. The decision made today may change tomorrow based on the market and customer dynamics.

Data is the new oil. Today, your company will fail if you are merely trying to deal with the data. Companies who can lead with data are up for success in the longer run. The security threat to our information and data cannot be determined. There is nothing confidential or secret. We have exposed all our personal and official information everything on the internet, knowingly or unknowingly by indiscriminately using social media platforms and mobile apps.

I am writing this chapter, when the entire world is hit by a deadly pandemic virus – COVID19 also known as Coronavirus. The whole world has come to a halt, and the human race is witnessing an unprecedented time. The origination of this virus was in Wuhan, China, and the first case was reported in December 2019 officially. 1.1 million people across the globe are already affected due to this deadly virus by the first week of April 2020.

After four months since its inception and spread, more than 60,000 people have succumbed to the deadly virus, and there is still no targeted treatment for this. While all the medical institutes, research, and think tanks are toiling on to find out a targeted therapy and vaccine, numbers are growing daily, and there is no precise prediction by when this exponential graph will start to flatten. Social distancing and lockdowns are the only precautionary steps that WHO (World Health Organization) and the governments of all nations are enforcing to break the spread and contamination chain. We are all locked inside our homes with access to only the essential needs of groceries and medicines. The workplaces and small-medium businesses are closed. The large-scale industries and manufacturing plants are locked down, impacting GDP forecasts of the nations and pushing them into significant recession. The IT companies are scrambling to support businesses in whatever way they can and trying to find out alternatives to help them.

All the businesses and company heads created the 2020 vision, growth plans, strategies, the 50-slider presentations with the roadmap to achieve targets and whatnot, that everything has gone for a toss. Sustaining the business during these unprecedented times has become a significant issue. People are losing jobs. Around 100 million people across the globe will lose their jobs by the end of 2020, as per the estimates. Approximately 3.5 million people have already filed for their unemployment insurance claims in the USA itself.

SMBs (Small Medium Businesses), which make 44% of the USA economy is down. The impact is so strong that the business continuity and disaster recovery plans of the companies have not worked out and have failed. The reason is that they had never considered work from home option, a mandate today, as an option earlier. The IT industry has struggled to a great extent as they are the enablers for other businesses that are entirely shut as of now. Though the IT companies scrambled initially for three to four weeks to enable engineers and set the pace for working from remote / home, things are stable for most of them now. Non-IT companies are facing hurdles to operate and support their businesses across all sectors and industries due to a significant drop in customer demand and restrictions implied for physical distancing.

The world we are in today is VUCA, i.e., full of Volatility, Uncertainty, Complexity, and Ambiguity. According to Nathan Bennett and G. James Lemoine (Harvard Business Review, 2014), this abbreviation was coined by the United States Army War College, describing the conditions resulting from the Cold War. Post that, many organizations in various industries have adopted it as a framework to determine their business & market challenges and plan the mitigation accordingly. The VUCA framework and analysis are used primarily in strategic, crisis, and disaster planning and management.

The volatility, uncertainty, complexity, and ambiguity characteristic in today's business world is the "new normal," and it characterizes difficult situations and conditions—volatility subjects to rapid and frequent change. The magnitude and the speed of the change are very disruptive and variable in a volatile situation. The outcome is unpredictable in this uncertain situation. Decision-making is difficult due to a lack of information and data.

Complexity resonates with the intricated issues and problems for which a solution is not readily available. There are also numerous moving parts, and they are interdependent due to which definitive decision making is difficult. Ambiguity is manifested in the absence of clarity and understanding of the situation. Ambiguity can also occur when there are multiple ways in which a piece of information is interpreted and perceived. Price fluctuation of the commodities due to geopolitical uncertainty or the Corona pandemic implications across the globe are few examples of the VUCA world. In short, VUCA epitomizes a chaotic and indeterministic world.

The VUCA framework helps to identify the unknown risks, issues, and consequences that are hard to anticipate through the usual risk assessment process. It then helps to recognize alternate paths to overcome challenging situations. It also helps to see if there are any business opportunities to tap into such circumstances instantly.

The skills and abilities that leaders possessed earlier are no longer beneficial in today's era as it lacks adaptability and agility in making and executing decisions. Strategic, logical, and critical thinking are the desired skills in a business leader that can make a difference.

Leaders who can lead in such a VUCA world can take their companies to the pinnacle of success and sustain in the market in the longer run. Leaders should be able to counter the VUCA-ness through their vision, clarity, decision making, and agility.

Now that we are clear on VUCA is, let me try and paint the VUCA world for a software or product development company.

Software development is a continuous problem solving and decision-making exercise throughout its life cycle. There is a lot of uncertainty and complexity in the entire process at different stages due to which there are challenges in choosing the right path and effective decision making at all points.

Let me paint the cacophonic madhouse of a software product development shop where there are uncertainties, complexities, and chaos.

The product that the engineering team working on is a highly complex one with multiple downstream, upstream applications and integral components. These 0components are written in different computer languages and technology stacks, which are a blend of old and new ones adding to the complexity. This blend is because the targeted customers need the product support on legacy technology with backward compatibility as they are yet to transition to the new technology stack. Different teams are supporting and working on these components, which have their own plan and roadmap without any joint alignment. They are all working in silos, without the common goal and calibration in the execution. There is no comprehensive development and monitoring plan shared between the teams.

Few of the frequently asked questions in an engineer's mind are

- *Should I upgrade to microservice architecture or leverage the monolithic one, which is already in use?*
- *Should I use Java, Golang, or .Net for coding?*
- *Should I use Kafka or MuleSoft for the message queueing in my feature?*
- *Which approach do I implement as we need to trade-off between the faster development or adhere to optimal design and architecture principles?*
- *Which non-functional requirement is associated with this feature? Is it scalability or performance?*

Minimum viable product with the basic features is already in production, and customers are actively using that. However, there are quality challenges in the production version of the product. It is full of bugs and issues due to which the organization is losing revenue and customers, impacting its revenues and brand equity. These issues are causing a high churn rate in the customer base of the company. They are complaining, frustrated, and leaving the product and the organization. There are negative feedback and critical comments all over the social media platforms for the product, especially on its terrible user experience. The customer-facing team has a hard time resolving and containing customer's rising concerns on the quality and usability of the product. Customers are actively looking for alternatives and are moving to the competitive products available in

14

the market as they feel that their concerns and issues are left unnoticed, with their feedback falling on deaf ears.

These are the standard questions that an engineer or a technical lead will have –

- *Which one is a priority out of so many defects?*
- *How should I proceed with fixing this critical defect when the details required for the investigation are missing?*
- *Should I do a quick fix to the problem or put a permanent fix as there are timeline implications on both?*
- *This incident is not a defect, so is this a new ask from the customer?*
- *Could this be a minor severity defect, but the customer is marking it as a critical?*
- *Is there a triaged and prioritized list of customer issues that the engineering team can focus on immediately?*

The remaining features of the product, slated to be released in production, are already delayed by a year. The scope of these new features is still unclear due to which the next steps and planning is not possible. Meanwhile, the team is scrambling to address all the production defects, shelled at them during the middle of their sprint in an unplanned manner, leaving them with no time to work on the planned new features and functionality. This unexpected work is causing considerable cost and timeline overrun for the company. Millions of dollars are already spent on the program, and further delays are impacting other plans and initiatives that are dependent on its completion in terms of timelines and budget. The other strategic initiatives for the company are either put on hold or cannot commence until this program is completed and released to the customers.

The scope of work and its definition is another challenge. Scope creep quite frequently in this unplanned work regime. There is no explicit listing of the requirements and user stories. One product owner wants 20 items, and the others have a list of 40 demands. There is also no alignment within the product management organization, causing conflicts within the product management organization. Internally, they both have a completely different understanding of the objective of the program and the set of requirements. The technical architects are worried about the technical debt, and enterprise architects are in an urgency to implement engineering excellence initiatives across the organization. They want to move to an entirely different architecture suitable for the product platform in the future. They also want to adopt a DevOps methodology and revamp the production deployment and release strategy at one go. The solution architect intends to safeguard the weakness and shortcomings in the third-party product integrated into the platform by proposing workarounds in other components & systems, compromising on the design principles.

Nobody has the insight to understand the product & business goals and tie it to the minimalistic features that need to be developed, to achieve it. Everything is a priority again here except for the customer's pain and their needs. The decision making in the product requirements are driven by the myopic attitude to have the same features built blindly in the new product platform that were present in the old legacy systems, to achieve the parity. The users do not want to leverage the recommended framework and standards in the new product. It is as good as asking for a touch-screen based smartphone, along with the button-pressing ability as well, that was available in the old mobile phones.

The dilemma for the project manager or the development manager in such scenarios are –

- *What is the prioritized list of the scope?*
- *What is the MVP, and is this aligned with all stakeholders?*
- *I do not have time for estimating the new features or stories as the sponsor wants to know the timelines of the entire project in the next two days. How do I create a schedule when there is no estimation?*
- *What about the risk in the solution when no design and reviews are happening?*
- *Should my team take up the customer feature first to develop or the technical debt or the production defect fix or the engineering excellence initiative?*
- *How should I plan the new work when more than half of my team's effort is going in ad-hoc and unplanned tasks?*
- *Which stakeholder's task is a priority as both are issuing a different set of requirements for the team to work?*

A laundry list of stakeholders in this program, and others are waiting to get this completed due to dependency. The program has multiple product owners, technical architects, solution architects, delivery, program, senior management, and sponsors. The challenge is not in having various stakeholders but in a lack of alignment between them when there is no single direction between enterprise and solution architects. The problem is when there is no alignment between product management and scrum teams, when there is no clarity on the ask from customer delivery, program, and senior management.

Delivery and program management needs to adhere to some timelines enforced on them. Executive management wants all the production defects to be fixed on priority, along with the adherence to the new development schedule. They refrain from getting aligned amongst themselves due to their intentions and interests, but they want all their asks addressed by engineering scrum teams on the highest priority. Some of them will not give guidance to the team to help them in their challenges, and some of them will be least interested in the program execution and the issues that are transpiring in it. But, they will always be at the forefront to provide their unsolicited and irrelevant opinions and suggestions. They will be the first to highlight their concerns in the larger forums to score brownie points.

The engineering manager will get lost in the stakeholder's web without having a clue on how to deal with it.

The questions rushing in the mind of the engineering manager are

- *Which stakeholder is essential, and who are the important ones?*
- *Does one stakeholder have the suggestion which is opposite to the other one? Which one should be considered?*

- *This stakeholder raises his voice pitch unnecessarily whenever we take something to him for his inputs or suggestions. But he is a key stakeholder. How to deal with him?*
- *This stakeholder should decide and take a stand, but he is not willing to and is not an active participant in the stakeholder discussion. How to deal with this situation?*
- *Different stakeholders ask for different or the same information on an ad-hoc basis at varying times. They need spoon-feeding on everything. How should I cater to this when I am not getting time to work on my engineering tasks?*

Interaction is entirely missing. While there is no central communication structure and plan present, it happens conveniently in silos and within the desired set of people or the stakeholders. The product owner provides the requirement to the scrum team on which they put their efforts only to realize after a couple of sprints of work that the other product owner does not require this. If at all they are aligned, then the design and the approach taken by the technical lead is incorrect without having the consent from the enterprise architect. Communication is only an on-need basis. Information is fetched by different stakeholders from random team members only to create confusion and angst. This randomness leads to incorrect data reporting. Some stakeholders have no clue about the project or details of it. They will try and hijack other meetings by asking questions that bring them up to speed, causing derailment of the meeting agenda and the objective. These stakeholders also add unnecessary follow-ups and wastage of time for everyone.

Team composition poses another challenge. There are engineers with different technical expertise and skillsets. It is a large team of approximately 30 engineers in geographically distributed locations in India and abroad. The working hours and differences in time zones add to the complexity of the program as they are not co-located. Out of all teams, few are outsourced to a third-party software organization that works on a contract basis. The scrum team contains a blend of team members from different locations, which makes it interesting and at the same time, a challenging combination of culture, mindset, and expertise. Individual team members have their own choice and preference to work on a specific module and technology. Some are vocal about it, and some are not. There are also issues when we have such diverse teams in terms of team dynamics and agreement. Lack of cultural sensitivity, communication, and listening competence add to the problems, notably when trust is missing amongst the team members.

Now, let us talk about the workload on the teams. The teams have been, on average, spending 12 hours daily to work on the other program that needs to be completed soon and to support business continuity by resolving production defects. It implies that the same scrum teams are working on both new feature development and production support. The committed stories planned at the start of the sprint are ignored as team members get pulled into calls and war rooms to troubleshoot production issues. There is no time left for anyone to take up work on new feature development. Tech debt and engineering excellence initiatives have become impossible, even to consider or discuss. The team's morale is at an all-time low; they are looking for opportunities outside, and are being pulled up by all stakeholders, resulting in a non-existent work-life balance. They do not have any personal time which they can spend with their families and friends, no time to pursue their areas of interest, or even have a 15-min water cooler chat with their office colleagues. The perception of the senior management for the team is not acceptable and is reflected in town-halls and forums. They neither receive any acknowledgment for their hard work and relentless efforts, nor do they see any growth for themselves in the organization. There is a high risk to the team sustenance in such an environment as they are dissatisfied, on the verge of quitting the product team and the organization.

We spoke about the product and the people. Now let us cover the processes. Process maturity is low in the organization. There are no well-defined processes for product development and engineering functions. Some teams are following agile, and the others, waterfall – tools used by engineering teams also vary for different groups. Some teams claim to be agile, and others are customizing and changing the agile principles and ceremonies to such an extent that there is no value left in following the methodology. There is no centralized mechanism to track anything. There is no central PMO (Program Management Office) function that can define and streamline common processes. The absence of a centralized PMO body results in disorganized and muddled execution of projects and programs. The project managers are allocated to a few projects and not all.

Documenting and recording particulars is not in the genetic makeup of the organization. Developing without appropriate documentation and reviews is something that most of the teams follow, due to which it causes conflicts, rework, and adds defects in the product. Documenting before and during coding is an overhead for the engineer, and will refrain from doing it most of the time. They do not realize the importance and how it will be of help to themselves when they must troubleshoot any defect or refer it to enhance the module further. It removes the dependency from the engineer who has built the element, to ease the transition to the new engineer who will be taking up in the future.

Lack of centralized knowledge repository on architecture, design, and implementation brings challenges to the team when it comes to fixing a production issue, and they scramble to get a quick relevant reference that can speed up the investigation and solution. There are also no defined engineering processes to improve code and product quality. Reviews for code and design are not mandatory and are also on-desire basis. If an engineer feels for a review, only then he or she gets it done. The production release mechanism is also different for different teams. There is no checkpoint or gate mechanism for the production release process. There are no release checklists before going for production release eventually missing and overlooking nook & corners, resulting in rollbacks. This release mismanagement causes terrible customer experience and wastage of effort.

The issue tracking and traceability metrics are not present, making it impossible for quick future reference. Data-driven discussion and decision-making are entirely missing. There is no uniformity in monitoring and reporting the project status. Different development and project managers create their templates for tracking and reporting causing inconsistency and discrepancy in the reports presented to senior and executive management.

There are multiple other challenges encountered in the product development ecosystem, which I have not captured in detail. Still, it impacts and slows down the speed of the development resulting in delayed time to market. Some of the issues include environment instability, lack of ownership, unaccountability & response-delays from third-party vendors and redundant meetings with no clear plan and objective. Lack of dedicated testing & mockup environment, information security constraints, inadequate quality checks, IT infrastructure dependency are few more addition to the list of challenges that we face in our daily product development regime.

If you have gone through the cacophony above, you will realize that there is one thing missing - One common goal. This dissonance and chaos are the results of the absence of one single purpose, and hence, there is no single direction, no alignment, and no focus. We are all over the place, and we are setting up for failure. No matter how much you try to fix these things individually or piece by piece, the program can never succeed without a common goal. There cannot be a perfect world carved out from the VUCA-ness of product development. Still, it can certainly improve, and this discord has to transform into a symphony for a healthy and sustainable ecosystem to deliver the right product for the customers.

On top of this complete madness, inadequate and timely decision-making ruins not only the development of the software but also the business. Taking decisions for software development is not easy compared to the ones that we make in our daily life. These decisions impact the company and the commercial viability of the product in the market. In the VUCA world, uncertainty and ambiguity primarily numb the ability to make timely and hard decisions.

Should we deliver the product faster, compromising on quality?

Engineering teams are always in a hurry to deliver more quickly without understanding if it is making sense to the customers and the business. Building faster cannot be the model or the basis of software development. It is undoubtedly essential for the success of it but provided, the consumption of the product is also at the same rate by the customers.

For example, you cannot release significant UI changes to an accounting software frequently, which is used by chartered accountants and tax professionals. These users are so used to the platform and product that they have been using for a long time that it becomes a part of them. They are habituated to it that the workflows and navigation on the screen are ingrained in their fingers. It is challenging for them to switch to a new UI or change the position of a button or sequence. Frequent release, in this case, will not help and may impact customer usability experience.

Another example is when the release timeline is just around the corner, and few features are lagging the intermediate milestones. The entire release will go for a toss impacting if the prompt decision is not made to drop these features or park it for the next release. The delay in decision-making will have implications on the projected revenues from product sales. The company will be forced to incur the loss of marketing, supply chain, and the shelf-reserving cost without any return on investment.

There are north goals that are set up by the business leaders of the organization, which is at 30,000 feet strategic level, but what gets missed is the way it gets translated into tactical strategy and effective execution. The vision and the goal of a company will remain unaccomplished if it is not orchestrated and delivered in the right manner at the ground level. Middle management should play a key role in acting as a liaison to translate the strategy into actions. Functions and teams should be aligned to the common goal with an operational execution plan and activity tracking. Appropriate steps and tough decisions should be taken to bring back the order to the development house so that the outcome is more predictable, aligned, and in sync with the financial goals of the company. In the end, what matters is the stakeholders and customers of the company. The company can grow, excel, and sustain if its stakeholders and customers are happy.

In my following chapters, I have tried to put forward my views on how we can bring the product development shop in order from chaos, bring in symphony and harmony from the cacophony by highlighting areas in which the appropriate actions and steps should be taken. These areas are fundamental to product development, but we, as an engineering team, tend to overlook and skip focusing on these aspects in our rush to solve technical problems and build faster solutions. There are certain places where I have shared some tips and tricks to make some of the changes and improvements quickly for faster results. It was challenging to cover all issues that we face because it may vary from product to product and company to company. Still, I have tried my best to cover the key fundamental aspects of software product engineering that need to be driven, composed, and orchestrated by the engineering leader.

Chapter 2

Comprehend the current dynamics and ecosystem

Sink vs. Swim

Now that you are amid the VUCA and chaotic software development world, and you are directionless, you should start from basics. It is the responsibility of you, as an engineering leader/manager, to get the house in order in a more systematic and streamlined way. You, as an engineering leader, will never be able to attain 100% success in transforming the house from chaos to order, considering the very characteristics of the VUCA system. But your target should be to achieve as much as you can to an extent where it starts bearing positive and desired results for the customers and the company.

The biggest challenge to be a leader in such situations is that the organization expects you to transform the way it is currently working without any guidance and support. There is no specific methodology or framework based on which you can drive the transition. There will be no prior knowledge or experience available in the organization who can provide guidance either. The "sink or swim" managerial approach is the most common approach that leaders take in such situations. Such situations are predominant in a more rapid-paced environment, like in software development companies. The companies use these conditions as testing waters to evaluate the leader's ability to manage and tackle the situation in the absence of any supervision. This management style focuses on a person's ability to get the task done without any guidance.

Managers and leaders who adopt this strategy have the right intentions most of the time, but they fail. Many high-potential leaders sink during this period due to the absence of support. It becomes extremely tough for leaders to navigate and sail in such situations as they are under immense pressure to show the results, without having a clue on the decisions made in the past. On top of that, he is yet to understand and assimilate the information dump on product issues, requirements, causes of delays, customer pain points, team dynamics, technology encounters, stakeholder expectations, and the list goes on. This initial phase of the new roles turns out to be daunting and vulnerable for leaders and managers as they must pave out a way to not only succeed but also develop the relationship network in the company from scratch.

Sail by learning

The best strategy for any new leader or the manager should be to learn first and then make decisions and changes. It is like sailing a boat. You must first learn to deal with the wind to sail. You can navigate your boat if you can gauge and learn about the wind speed, the wind direction, and the pressure it creates on the sail. A low-pressure zone in front and the high-pressure zone is created behind the sail. The boat accordingly moves into the low-pressure area and moves forward due to the force created by the difference of the pressure. The sailor must hold and direct the sails based on the intended path of the boat. He should know the course in which he intends to lead the boat, the wind path, and the difference of pressure mechanism working on the sails of the boat.

Similarly, the leader or the manager should first learn the critical aspects of the product and the ecosystem before he/she is ready to lead the development of it. You cannot learn to sail just by reading some books or watching a few videos on it. You will discover only by doing it, by trying on a small sailboat before venturing into the sea on a more massive ship. He should have better control over every facet that comes under his circle of influence to be able to sail better. For that, you should learn first, perform small things, and again learn from the results of it. This cycle of 'doing by learning' should be on a constant roll, and that will empower you with better decision making to navigate through the rough waters of the software product development. This approach will make you stronger in changing the direction, perform critical maneuvers without tipping off.

Listen and Understand

Gaining people's confidence and trust should be the first and foremost strategy for you. You need to be on the listening and observing mode because any immediate steps or actions by you, without due diligence, are prone to flop. It can have a drastic impact on the results and harm your role and image, as you are under constant scrutiny. The best way to approach is to connect and collaborate with the team and stakeholders to understand and grasp as much as you can. Then, take baby steps in alignment with the team and small wins in the initial stages so that you gain confidence in your decisions, including others as well. The stakes are significant in any multifaceted program with high visibility. Hence, you should refrain from making any substantial changes in a hurry without having a complete understanding and grip on it. You might be tempted to fix some of the apparent gaps that you see, but you need to know the reason why this was not fixed earlier by the previous manager if it is so evident. Your every step is under watch, and once the impression created, it will last for a good long time. That is why your strategy should be to communicate and listen more and more.

There are a few things you should take care of while having interactions with other players within the organization. Information will be exploded to you from the team, colleagues, vendors, and stakeholders. Most of this information will make no sense to you initially, as you do not have the background. That is perfectly fine. You will understand it gradually with the time and more you get involved in the details. But you should make it a point to capture key points and notes during all your discussions. It will help you to refer it in the future, connect the dots, and derive meaningful insights. You should try to understand the implicit points and the underlying message, especially the pain points during your discussions.

Know the big picture

Start from the top to bottom approach. You cannot make a change unless you understand the vision and goal of the function/company. Plan your interactions with the leadership and engineering heads to understand the strategic vision of the group, stipulated time horizon

30

to achieve it, and the potential roadblocks and challenges that they foresee. You should be well-versed with the roadmap of the product that they want to launch, along with its targeted customer segment and the revenue & profitability numbers that the company wants to achieve. These insights will give you an idea of the entire boundary at a high level that you will need to focus on. With this, you should also have a fair understanding of the company's and engineering organization structure, governance model, and the processes at a high level.

Knowing how the front line and supporting functions integrate with the engineering is also vital. You should understand the product-associated sales and marketing plan, their milestones in terms of go to the market and their expectation on the specific product feature that they are planning to put across as value proposition to the customers. The product's business model, in terms of investment, third-party integrations, vendors, and pricing should also be known to you. The point of contact of each function should be on your speed dial and contact list. These details will give you a gamut of the product ecosystem and operating model that you will be in charge and leading.

Once you have the strategic view about the product, the next step is to dive into the tactical part of it. Identify the vital goals that are strategically aligned with your product roadmap. These are the goals that need your maximum concentration. You need to build your strategy to accomplish these goals. You will be unable to give attention to all of them at the same time, and that is why prioritization is essential. Prioritize the list of goals, in the ascending order of its completion time, goals that are relatively less complex and will take less time to complete should be on the top of the list. The following ones should be more complex and time-consuming to achieve.

Small and quick wins are always right and less risky. The overall timeline to accomplish the goals, for you, should be well before the expected schedule by the board and the leadership. Your strategy should be detailed out with intermediate milestones like a 30-60-90-day plan and work relentlessly to achieve them. But again, all of this is still at a high level. It needs to be broken down further into actionable tasks with clear completion/success criteria.

Who has stakes in the product?

It is time to know the people around you, especially those who have stakes in your product and the program. They have a particular interest in your product. Stakeholder analysis is the next step after you get the big picture of the strategic vision and the goals for the product at a high level. You cannot succeed and win in your project unless you have the support from your stakeholders. Stakeholders could comprise of the project team, company management, executives, sponsors, shareholders, customers, and product users. They are the ones who have invested in the product either in terms of money or efforts. The outcome of the project impacts the stakeholders. It can be reversed way as well. They can also affect the development course or the execution strategy midway based on their inputs and influence.

You have to deal and collaborate with this set of people more often during the product development journey. You should know their role, impact, and influence on the product development & program. Understanding their specific areas of interest and your dependency on them, if any, are critical to the co-ordinated and successful execution of the program.

Resource vendors and third-party contractors who are contributing to the product development, in some way, are also the stakeholders of the project. The sellers, supply chain brokers and partners, media houses, e-commerce providers, etc. are also included as part, if you are dependent on them for the selling of your product. You should come up with the entire list of stakeholders and sort it in the descending order of their impact, interest, and influence in the product.

You should have insights on the contribution made in the past, by them to the product and possibly, shades of their behavior too from the previous manager and colleagues. There are always few stakeholders who are tough to manage, and you should keep them on the top of your list. These stakeholders can hijack your entire development plan, taking away most of your time to fulfill their asks and overwhelm you with enormous pressure unnecessarily. Knowing a bit about their behavior and expectations will equip you better to deal with them effectively.

Understand team composition, acknowledge their problems

You should now start your meetings with your team. You should work and interact with them cohesively to get firsthand information and experience about their working style and challenges that they face. You must have 1:1 discussion with each of your team members and understand their skillsets, technical areas of expertise, their work assignment, and the difficulties that they are facing in their day to day work.

Seek their views and suggestions in terms of how you can help them in removing some of the roadblocks that they face. You need to earn the trust of the team as a leader, as they will have their doubts and will be skeptical initially. You should be honest and transparent with them so that they believe in you as a leader. One thing you should practice as well as make your team clear is, the leader/manager is the servant of the team and not the other way. The manager's success or failure is entirely dependent on the team's success or failure. The manager is not the boss of the group, but he is one amongst themselves. It is one family.

Every team member is different in their way of thinking, working, communicating, and analyzing things. As a leader, you should be able to harness the best of each team member, leverage them with the right work and opportunity so that they shine like superstars. Your team is the actual workforce on the ground. They will provide a plethora of insights to you on how to build an excellent reliable product. You just need to acknowledge their views & efforts, assist with all the help,

34

and remove all other noise and hindrances that are in their path. You will get to hear the problems and issues from all your stakeholders and related parties in the program, but it will be only your team who can provide you insights on the cause of those issues and suggest potential steps to address them.

In your meetings with product management, business stakeholders, leadership, or engineering head, you will often get to hear that the customers are very critical and upset about our product as there are many issues and defects in it. They are rightfully raising their concerns time and again with you as they expect you to turn this around. The product management will harp on the high turnaround time that the team takes to fix a critical defect that impacts its sprint velocity and overall productivity. But you will get to know the cause of these issues only from the team members. The team might not have got enough time to work and come up with a design before the development due to unrealistic timeline pressure. Or they might have been bombarded with unplanned tasks by the product management in the middle of the sprint leading to additional time for fixing the critical defect. Or the team themselves skipped the design and review steps in a hurry to implement the functionality and delivered it, due to lack of discipline. The root cause could be many, but the outcome is the buggy product. These issues and the root cause of it is something that you need to understand and make a note of it.

Product architecture and design

In simple words, product architecture is the amalgamation of the functional elements in such a way that their interaction and working provides the desired output to the users and customers. Product architecture should be robust and flexible in terms of scaling it to futuristic needs with minimal changes in the code. It plays a pivotal role as it forms the chassis of the product. As an engineering manager, you should be well versed in the product architecture and its design that you will be leading. You should get the entire architectural overview and design walkthroughs from the product architect and the technical leads in the team. You should also know the internal and external integration points within and with other components outside the product.

A product suite or the platform contains a wide range of technologies to build the integral elements. There are reasons behind using a specific technology over others for a component, and you should be aware of them. The more you have the command on the architecture/design, the more it empowers you to have logical and concrete discussions with product management on any specific needs. It also puts you in a comfortable spot to make practical decisions on the technical course of the product. You are not expected to know each nook and corner of the design, but you should certainly be aware of the big picture. You can always rely on your technical leads for any specific in-depth information. Instead, you should spend effort and time in understanding the gaps and technical debt that is present in the current design of the product.

- *Is there any technical backlog that is being maintained by the team?*
- *And what is the percentage of the technical debt that is addressed by the team in each sprint?*
- *Is the product management aligned to solve technical backlog along with the new features?*

These are some of the crucial questions for which you should have clarifications from your technical leads and product management.

Assess the documentation

In parallel, you should make it a point to go through the product documentation, project-related artifacts, or wiki that is available. There will always be a very handful of folks who will be contributing in terms of documentation and enriching the knowledge repository. Most of them consider it as an overhead and burdened when they are expected to document anything. You should go through the list of open issues, both reported by customer and product management in the backlog. These details will educate you in terms of defect types and faulty components that are impacting the customer experience. Also, the documentation will let you know the quality and the depth at which the team does the analysis and due diligence before they start working on it. The quality of the inbound work description matters a lot.

You should go through the sample stories and tasks in JIRA created for your team by-product management / other teams and notice the level of details that they provide in them. Whether or not it contains a clear and detailed description of the task with an acceptance criterion. The absence of this information and non-compliance of the process also brings in ambiguity in work. The repercussions may not be immediately known, but they will surface at a later point, making it more costly to address. Make it a point check and validate your understanding with your critical team members at every step.

Quality of the product, development methodology and work fulfillment process

Once you have the big picture on the vision for the product, the team composition, architecture, and design of the product, you can now deep dive into the next level on how the requirements flow in for the engineering team and the process they employ to fulfill them. There are multiple points that you need to dig and understand.

- *Is there a dedicated product owner for the product or is shared among multiple products?*
- *Channel used to direct the requirements from business to engineering? in the form of emails, excels, ad-hoc requests, JIRA epics/stories, or verbally without any documentation.?*
- *Is there a definite success criterion identified at the start of each requirement, or are they unknown till the end?*
- *What is the level of detail provided for each requirement? Is it granular enough for engineering?*
- *Is there a traceability matrix managed for the requirements during the development lifecycle?*

The development procedure & framework followed by the team and the conformance maturity to that process.

- *Does the team follow the waterfall, agile, or abused agile methodology where they have tweaked everything as per their needs and convenience?*
- *What is the due diligence done to understand and groom the requirement before commencing the implementation?*
- *Is the story broken and estimated?*
- *Do team prototype requirements that are unclear at the start and get it validated by the customers and product management?*
- *Are the demos planned and done at the end of the sprints?*
- *Do the test engineers get involved from the start or at the end of the story development?*
- *Are the design and code reviews done, and to what extent and frequency?*

The monitoring and reporting of the requirements and quality are equally important as the product development. The engineering stakeholders rely heavily on the progress report, and timely status updates w.r.t. feature completion and defect convergence.

- *Are there any metrics specific to code, quality, and deployment tracked and monitored?*
- *Does the team take up automation testing of the story/tasks?*
- *How much is the product management aligned with taking up technical debt and quality improvement tasks.?*

- *Is there a test framework followed to identify the test scenarios and test cases?*
- *Does the team follow any coding best practices/checklist for better code quality?*

And the list goes on. The steps that the developers follow to test and check-in their code in the central code repository. The environment and infrastructure used by the engineering team and the protocol or gates that they use for code promotion before production releases.

If the team is working in a sprint-based model, you should fetch the data points on the metrics related to the productivity of the team. The last six sprints (3 months) data should be enough to gauge on how the team has been doing in terms of delivering the work. For that, you need to backtrack the velocity of the sprint, their planned vs. delivered ratio, and the spillovers that they are doing sprint over sprint. The reasons for the overflow is essential to note to address its root cause. The root cause could be many, for example, over-commitment in the sprint compared to the capacity, or random addition of new work in the middle of the sprint. The inappropriate estimation of the work taken in the sprint resulting in taking additional time to complete than anticipated is also a potential cause for the spillage.

The composition of work in each planned sprint also makes a difference. The ratio of planned vs. unplanned work, the production defects, and the new functionality work should be known as well. These numbers will help you in setting the priority of the backlog and the sprint. With this, you will see the time team is spending on working unplanned vs. planned tasks so that it can be much better organized in the future, if those tasks are of business priority. The visibility to the stakeholders on the type of work assigned to the team is also crucial, especially in the way it is communicated to them.

Quality should be of supreme importance to any engineering function and product development organization. You need to know the quality of the product that your team is working on, the process that the team follows to produce the right quality code, and the measurement criteria for it. You should make a point to collect customer pain points and views on the product, if it is already in production.

Customers nowadays are very vocal if the product is sub-standard and lacks quality. They post their views on social media platforms and other public forums. You should collect insights from these platforms on the pain points of the customers w.r.t. your product usage. You should obtain this information from sales and customer servicing teams as it will be readily available with them. You should also check the backlog of the defects, logged by your test engineers over the period that has remained unattended. You should make a note of the top critical defects, based on your analysis, from the functional and non-functional standpoint. Get these shortlisted defects validated by your product management and technical leads, to confirm that they are ones causing maximum problems in the product.

There are many non-functional requirements (NFR) that might apply to your product and functionality based on the usage and the data volume of the customer/users. Performance, usability, security, resiliency, reliability, supportability, extensibility, etc. are some examples of NFRs to be tested against the set benchmark before released in the production. You need to check with your test engineers about the test strategy that they apply to validate these NFRs. The type of test data used for the testing and the source of it. There could be various ways to generate the test data, and you should know the way that your team takes to create and test the flows.

- *Does the testing team validate these NFRs in separate performance environments or the same lower environment along with functional testing?*
- *Is the test data created using stubs, or the masked sample data from production?*

The responsibility of quality does not rely only on the test engineers. The developers also have the accountability to make sure that the quality is not compromised. You should understand the steps that developers take to ensure they build a good quality code.

- *Do the developers write unit test cases, and what is the code coverage?*
- *Does the team use any static analysis tool to keep a check on quality?*
- *Do they get their code reviewed before they submit it to the code repository?*
- *Are there any guidelines that the team follows to enforce secured coding practices and maintain standards?*
- *Does the team assess other code parameters like structural complexity, code smells, duplication, vulnerabilities, etc.?*

- *Does the bug triage happen with the testing and product management team?*

You should be aware of the turnaround time taken by the engineers to fix a defect and type of testing done on the fix by the developer and the tester.

- *Is the defect fixing done in the same sprint or the next one?*
- *Does the team use any third-party tools to perform security and performance testing?*
- *Does the team automate test cases and scenarios?*
- *Is there any automation roadmap that they follow?*
- *What is the percentage of automation vs. manual?*

You should be aware of the testing depth & rounds done on single new functionality developed before releasing it to the customers.

The answers to all the above questions are required and to be understood. That will give you a perfect idea of how the team currently does the work, the form in which the product needs come to the engineering team, the steps that they follow to build it, and finally deliver it. These pieces of information are very crucial as it forms the basis for your product engineering that will have a direct influence on the quality and time to build the product. These internal engineering areas may not sound or look critical to you at first. Still, they can turn into high-risk items eventually and potentially failing your path to achieve the goal if it is not addressed and set in the right way. I consider them as nuts, bolts, and belts of the engineering machinery that should be in good shape, monitored, and maintained at a regular frequency to ensure it works smoothly in a harmonized manner.

Governance and reporting

Governance, the meaning as per the Oxford dictionary, is the action or manner of governing a state, organization, etc. and the controls that are in place. In software product development parlance, governance is all about monitoring, measuring, and management of the product. The parameters to be monitored varies according to the stage of the product development.

The leader or the manager needs to know if there is any governance structure followed in the program. The metrics used to monitor the status & progress of the development, overall reporting structure, channels through which the progress is shared with stakeholders, and the cadence of reporting.

We also covered some areas earlier in this chapter, to be governed in terms of requirement matrix, design, code quality, functionality demos, test strategy, NFRs, documentation, defects, stakeholders, team productivity, etc. during the product development phase. The critical point to know the ways it is administered and tracked actively. Other metrics are dependent on these and whether those are analyzed and derived from the governance monitoring.

- *Does the team track on the type of work they turnaround every sprint, i.e., feature development vs. technical debt?*
- *Is there a process followed to identify risks and issues that might crop up during the product development lifecycle?*

- *Does the leadership do program review?*
- *Does the program has a governance structure and an escalation matrix?*

These are the questions to which answers need to be sought and understood. The process of product development is one aspect. Still, effective monitoring and evaluating the progress from time to time is equally important to ensure that the team and the work are on course with better predictability.

After this elaborate and exhaustive information gathering & learning exercise, the next step is to start putting some action plans. You should identify top things to be addressed on priority. Securing early wins in the right way is critical during this transition period. You may tempt to take up all the reforms and changes at the same time on your plate, but that will not allow you to focus each shift in depth. Too many things at the same time may have disastrous results. You should take up only 2 – 3 items at a time and put arduous efforts to make that change a success through flawless execution.

While bringing about change, you may fell prey to cultural inadaptability. There are different ways in which organizations manage their cultural diversity. The expectation and definition of certain things vary as the culture and with the global teams in today's world, this is very common. The change that you want to bring in should not be an individual win or an accomplishment but rather a team pursuit to get better and better.

In the next chapters, we will cover some critical zones that should be addressed along with your team to transform your chaotic product development shop into an ordered one with harmony and symphony. You should plan your changes in small waves so that the planning and the execution are in better control for everyone. These small waves should be marked with the intermediate milestones to monitor the progress and time taken to achieve it. The results of each change should be investigated and tracked over a period to check its effectiveness. The deep learning exercise that you underwent to learn about the product, and the company will certainly set you in the right direction and pace your executions.

In this transformation path, there could be ways where you can achieve impressive results by manipulation and dishonesty. But, that path will not last for long. You should never set a wrong example for your team, peers, and the company and yourself; instead, they should look up to you as a Change and Transformational Leader who has the desire and the spine to make some hard decisions for the benefit of the product and the company. You should never let the means undermine the end results. The transformation will reap you the desired results only if there is a behavioral and mindset change, along with the operational effectiveness in the team to attain the quantifiable business objectives.

Chapter 3

Customers don't want to buy a quarter-inch drill. They want a quarter-inch hole

Customer centricity should be in the genetics of any product organization. Research has shown that 72% of new product and services innovation fails to deliver on expectations. It implies 7 out of 10 products are outright rejected by the customers as soon as they are launched. Failure to understand customer needs and fixing a non-existent problem are the primary reasons for these products and services to fail.

Salesforce's "State of the Connected Customer" report highlights that 73% of customers expect companies to understand their needs and expectations, but only 51% believe companies generally do. Similarly, 62% of customers expect companies to adapt based on their actions and behaviors, but just 47% believe companies do.

Earlier, the organizations adopted the approach in which they will build the product and services based on inputs within the organization, typically from the sales team. Then the sole strategy is to sell the product and services to as many customers as they can. They want to try and capture as much market as they can. The pricing strategy revolves around commoditization models where they will provide discounts, offers, or at a lesser price. It is done to achieve as many sales as possible.

This entire approach lacks value that the customer is looking for in the product. Such companies can witness a surge in sales initially, but it cannot be sustained for a longer time as they will be beaten up by their competitors in the same space,which will bring in differentiation and value in their product and services. The pricing may be high compared to others, but they will charge for the premium and value that they bring on the table for the customers.

This outlook is changing now. Organizations and decision-makers in them understand the expectation and the behavior of the customers now. With the boom in social media platforms, customer analytics techniques, decision-makers are now well equipped with the information and feedback almost real-time from their customers that they can leverage to make decisions and alterations, to add value to the product.

Customer is everything for any organization, business, or company. The company's success depends on its customers. There will be neither sales nor revenue without customers, and hence they need to be the focal point in your strategy. For any business to succeed, all the functions should align and work to achieve common customer goals that are laid by the company board and the strategy team. There should be complete alignment between these functions and within those functions.

Better relationship & trust with clients, enhancing customer satisfaction, and increasing the success of your patrons can be achieved by putting them at the center point in whatever you do. Ideas flow better, and work is more productive when you connect and support your customers. You also feel good about your accomplishments, and the success of your clients will invariably drive your success.

There are multiple functions in an organization that works towards the goal of creating products and services and deliver them on time. Sales, marketing, product, user experience, and engineering, all drive towards the strategic objectives of the organization. However, the challenge on the ground is that these functions only want to meet timelines and targets set by the management. It eventually takes off their focus from the customer needs. The sales team's priority is to convert the sales pitch by just selling the product; marketing will be busy highlighting the differentiation of the product and engineering in a crazy rush to build the functionality that product management has asked. In this entire ecosystem, the focus on customer needs, which is the essence, is lost, ending up in a sub-optimal product for them.

It is not as simple as many would think by merely saying that 'customer is everything' or 'customer is always right,' customer-centric culture would be imbibed. It is quite challenging to keep the customer in the center and plan, align your strategy according to it. The other challenge is that customer needs always change, and it is challenging to keep pace with it. Different functions and verticals within the company also need to align and work towards the benefit of the customer.

The key to achieving customer focus is the shift in the mindset. Typically, the engineering teams have the vendor mindset, which means to focus on the deliverable that is being set by the product owner and the manager, building & delivering the product rather than ensuring that it is solving customer problems or meeting their needs or not. Instead, the team should have a *partnership mindset* that involves and validates with the customer continually throughout the product development journey. It helps to value customer needs & problems better and also to understand its implication on their business.

The customer-centric engineering approach should be adopted as it adds value to the organization in several aspects. It helps to contain and reduce the level of risk in a new product or feature development. At the concept stage itself, you need to get it validated by the customer. Also, the expectation from the product management is to do a complete market study and research in terms of how other providers and competitors deliver the same feature or product. Such research provides the engineering team with insights and ideas to design a smarter solution with differentiation.

Customer-centric engineering helps to bring down the cost of the company in terms of product development. If the team is in alignment with the customer on the requirement at the concept and development phase itself, then the probability of adding error in the product minimizes to a great extent. It significantly decreases the rework on the product at the later stages, which becomes very costly then. Customer buy-in on the concept and the prototypes at the early stages of the product development also provides confidence not only to the customers but also to the engineering team. They are more assured of their approach, can focus and deliberate in detail to implement it successfully.

Alpha and Beta testing in a customer-mimicked environment or customer's test environment helps to identify the reliability and performance issues upfront so that they can also be addressed before the production rollout. It also helps in minimizing the cost impact and post-sales service requests.

The typical impression of the product development team is that they just want to hit the delivery milestones, build features and products, fix defects, release new versions, and do some cool technical stuff & experiments. I would concur with this to a certain extent. The primary reason is the engineering mindset and the management expectation from the team. Their productivity and performance are measured based on the engineering tasks and yardsticks that they have achieved.

There is no dedicated focus from the company on the other aspects of the engineering team and the ways to build and groom it. For example, analytical ability, communication skills, business acumen, domain knowledge, and process compliance are the critical aspects in software engineering but never paid heed to enhance it. No doubt, this becomes the responsibility of the company leadership and the culture that they have adopted. Still, it is the responsibility of the engineering leader and manager to ensure that the team is continuously coached and trained in all these areas along with technology.

Right Hiring

Hiring the right set of people is key to the overall success of an engineering function. Typically, we evaluate the candidate on its technical knowledge and hands-on with bare minimum communication proficiency. But that is not enough to build a customer-focused engineering team. The candidate needs to be a team player with excellent listening and communication skills. The person should have the command in the thought process and should be able to articulate his point of view with clarity. The person should have an understanding of the business and should be able to tie on how the technical changes and features in a product impact the business outcomes. He/she should be able to highlight the business value that he has brought in the past assignments done by him.

The candidate should be smart in steering the conversation and, at the same time, be sensitive to the thoughts and views of the others. Such candidate will play a crucial role in building the relationship and trust with the customers and stakeholders. Such engineers will be proficient in articulating the need for a change in the product and its implication to the customer business, to the other team members. Candidates who are good at just completing their assignments are not good enough. They should go beyond their commitments and take up additional tasks and ownership whenever they see an opportunity. Now, this can be evaluated by knowing his interests, especially what further learning and training he/she is doing at his own time and own dime. Is the candidate subscribed to a tech community where he contributes? This way, you can have a better view of the candidate's personality and his / her focus towards the career.

Attention to detail

Groom your engineers not only in building the right products but also to possess attention to detail. I always take this example whenever I speak to my team members on why attention to detail is essential.

The space shuttle Columbia disintegrated, killing its crew of 7 astronauts on 1st Feb 2003 while re-entering into the earth's atmosphere. After investigation, it deduced that a small piece of the foam insulation had chipped from one of its fuel tanks, hitting the left-wing of the space shuttle during the launch. This little piece of foam damaged the protective tiles meant for protecting the shuttle during the re-entry in the earth's atmosphere from the hot gases and massive heat. The tiles failed, spawning a chain of reactions leading to the disintegration. This tiny piece of foam costed seven lives and destruction of the multi-million technology marvel.

- *Foam piece size - 13 x 15 x 4 inch*
- *Shuttle size: 184 x 78 x 57 feet*
- *Foam piece weight - 0.75 kg*
- *Shuttle weight: 8000 lb*

Later, mockup tests proved that a piece of foam weighing as small as just 19.8 grams could repeat the Columbia disaster.

Software engineers should have the ability to achieve thoroughness, think through all possible angles, and complete tasks with much higher accuracy. Initially, to train the team, you might want to create a checklist for the smallest items to ensure that they are not missed or overlooked at the required time. Such checklists are built and evolved over some time from the learnings and experience in the past. Train the team to take notes while having brainstorming and discussions with customers or within the group.

Mind mapping is an excellent framework that can help team members to collate their thought clutter on a whiteboard that can be knit together to build a compelling use case, feature or a story.

Defect injection is a vital metric to evaluate and gauge the attention and thoroughness done by an engineer while implementing the story. There are people, who by nature, are gifted in systematically organizing and planning their work, but with many, it is not. Hence, as an engineering manager, you should plant initial checks and balances to ensure minor things are not missed out, that might spawn undesired surprises later.

Train beyond the role

Training is vital to make an engineer business-driven and customer-focused. The industry norm is the training programs are restricted to the role and the job description of the engineer. Training will be provided only in technology confined to the work that he or she is currently doing, or anticipated in the future. Engineers are not expected to get trained in their working domain and the industry vertical. Hugely few companies invest in an overall training program for an engineer. They are also not trained in communication, listening, soft & behavioral skills, and cross-cultural sensitivity. These skills play a pivotal role when an engineer is interacting and working with clients directly. It adds a lot of value when they work in cross-cultural, diverse, and geographically distributed teams. They are more polished and fluent in their communication, articulation, equipped with the domain knowledge.

Training should be beyond their roles and responsibilities. They should be well versed in their company business model and the products that they offer in the market. They should know their customer segment and how the company helps its customers, the distribution channels for the product, the feedback mechanism, and to some extent, the pricing models as well. There should be focussed trainings to teach customer interactions and nuances of it. They must know the dos & don'ts to take care, especially when they are interacting with them, co-located at client locations. They should be aware and sensitive in terms of culture, diversity, race, and ethnicity. Engineers with such competence become the brand ambassadors of their companies and create WOW factor for their customers.

Customer-centric product development

From the engineering/leader perspective, you should strive to build customer-focused engineering teams. The concept is straightforward. The process that the engineering team takes up to create any software or the product should solve customer problems and meet their requirements. It is possible only when this customer focus approach is followed through the entire development lifecycle, right from concept to design to build to support phase of the product. The customer should be in the center while carving out the business goals and underlying processes. Research says that businesses can be approximately 30 – 40% more profitable if there is customer concentration throughout the engineering and support cycle of the product.

There must be a structured approach to the entire product development cycle. Maximum time should go in the early stage - requirement brainstorming, conceptualization, storyboarding, and design phase. Once the use cases and flows are sketched out, then it takes much less time to implement it. Teams should avoid haste & hurry to implement the half-baked solution as it will lack critical use cases for the customers and will be more error-prone.

Here are a few steps to be followed to identify the problems of the customers, pain-points and design a relevant and useful product for them.

1. Explore the current situation of the customer. It can be done by creating a step-wise flow from the user perspective in a storyboard format and write down user narratives. The goal is to gather information on the current situation in terms of the steps the customers follow, any tools that they use, frequency of using those tools, time taken, workarounds, types of users, expectations, pain points, cost, etc. It will give you an understanding of the moves that the user chooses to meet its needs and the pain points they face in that route.

2. 70% of the purchasing decisions are taken to solve a particular problem. Identify the problem (the need), user's desires, emotions, and context with which they use the product. Knowing these decision drivers is crucial. There are several frameworks and techniques used by the sales team to get insight into these drivers. One of the persuasive techniques used across is Toyota's '5 Whys' method in which you keep repeating whys until the problem, and the probable solution becomes clear. Understand the implications of these problems comprehensively that customer is facing in terms of brand, business, emotional, social or market perspective. It is a very crucial step as it sets the basis for carving out the solution to the problem.

3. Rank order the problematic areas of the customer in terms of priority. Tagging them into distinct needs (asked explicitly by the customer) and implicit requirements (derived from the conversation and analysis) will help in categorizing and prioritizing, done by customer engagement and product management groups. But, in reality, the engineering team do not get requirements only from product management, there are other stakeholders, including customers who provide their list of necessities as well. Enterprise architecture teams have their own set of requirements that needs to considered in the product development cycle. It may be to address technical debts, migration to new platforms/technology, or do fundamental design & architectural changes in the product to make it more scalable. Marketing group might have their demand to add certain features in the product to capture details of the customer, to cross or up-sell opportunities in the future. Collate all these

requirements from all sources and bucket them accordingly, as per the priority by-product management. It will help the engineering team to plan better and work on them as and when required, directed by the product owner.

4. If the product is already in place, then identify the features of your product and map it to the pain points of the customers, which will help in alleviating and solving it for them. There could be additional features or improvements to be developed in the product. Some companies have multiple channels in the form of social media and other online platforms to seek continuous feedback from their customers and users. There is a dedicated customer support team that collates the input and passes it to the product management so that they can put them in the backlog and prioritize it for engineering teams. Not many organizations are matured in seeking real-time customer inputs. The ones who does it continuously and strive for the product enhancement helps them to keep up with the pace of changing customer needs. It eventually helps in increasing the top line and bottom line for the company.

5. Design and build the product/features with the value proposition around it. It will not only help in solving the problem of the customers but also create differentiation and stickiness for the product in the market. A value proposition is a statement that gives clarity to the prospects and customers of what your product will deliver, how it will benefit them, and why the prospects should buy from you and not from your competitors. It helps the company to make a strong impression of their product in the

minds of the customers. A value proposition is not a tag line or punch line shown in the advertisements; it is that differentiation the product brings on the table for their customers, which the competitors in the market don't provide. Determining the value proposition is an extensive exercise and is mostly managed by the marketing and sales function of the company.

6. Validate the functionality in terms of POC (Proof Of Concept) with the early adopters or volunteered customers. They will provide instantaneous feedback to the product and engineering teams if they are in the right direction or not. It also helps to win customer's trust, and they consider themselves an integral part of the product development process. It is a recommended practice to share and highlight the features with the prospects and customers that are on the roadmap for the team in the future. It ensures fruitful collaboration with no element of surprise to both the customers and product/engineering teams. The more proactive you are on communication with your customers, the more it helps in terms of understanding their feedback and the pulse of the market. Trust is the key, and to earn it, you should focus on solving customer's problems before they get frustrated and start impacting the business.

The above steps not only help in deriving the usability, prioritization, and design of the product but also makes the execution, pricing, and go-to-market more straightforward with less risk.

Mostly, product and sales teams are involved in identifying the pain points and the respective solutions, and the final list is passed on to the engineering without providing customers or any business context.

Instead, the engineering team should be an active participant in understanding customer pain and needs so that they can appreciate the functionality they are building for them. It also drives the engineers to solve their customer problems with more rigor, creating a difference and WOW factor for them.

Once the product is created and delivered to the customer, customer service comes into play, which is pivotal in customer retention. The engineering squad should never lose the sense of urgency in incorporating customer-pointed enhancements. Settling for good is not enough; instead, the team should aim for a great and steadfast customer alliance.

Typically, there are two ways in which the customer problems are addressed. One is that the company constitutes a multi-level support function where the quick concerns, queries, and issues faced by the customer/user is addressed by the on-call level support over the phone or email. The SLA (Service Level Agreement) for this level is very small, as they are expected to solve customer concerns within a short time. If the issues are more complex, in the product or something that will take time for investigation, then the problem is routed to the next level. This level has a higher SLA time as the fix to the problem would take more time to code and test. You can see this support function structure in more mature product and service organizations. The alternate way which the company employs is to have the scrum team itself solve the customer concerns and production issues. Now, this becomes difficult when the same scrum team is asked to address the production issues and perform new feature development as well.

If your organization has adopted the second approach, then you can dedicate 15% to 20% bandwidth of your scrum team to support and fix production defects. You can also place your team members on rotation every sprint so that everyone gets the experience and opportunity to maintain & support production concerns. The teammate who is on-call for the production support should be monitoring the vital parameters and health of the product and be available as soon as the customer reports an issue. The recommended practice is to have at least two colleagues who should do the support and on-call so that they can fill in for each other, and it does not become overwhelming for anybody. The rotation policy balances out the workload and stress evenly within the team.

Organizations will not succeed if they confine themselves to the above processes only. There should be measurable data and continuous analysis, almost real-time to check if the steps and process change is having the desired impact on your customers or not. Hence customer-specific metrics become an implicit need in today's world to gauge the product performance in the market and have more realistic business and financial forecast. Revenue and growth numbers merely will not give you that insight. There are specific customer-specific metrics that product organizations should capture and monitor frequently.

One of the most popular parameters is NPS (Net Promoter Score). This metric is an index that ranges from -100 to 100 and indicates the overall sentiment towards your product and brand. Many such parameters can be used to measure customer sentiment about your product. More important is to share these details and metrics to the engineering teams at regular cadence so that they understand it and work towards improving it. Such business visibility is key to the engineering function as they need to have the essential business acumen which should be laying the foundation and prove handy when they are making any decisions and working on the product.

As Harvard Business School Professor Theodore Levitt had said, "People don't want to buy a quarter-inch drill. They want a quarter-inch hole!" which I find extraordinarily relevant and accurate today considering the rapid change in consumer behavior impacting the market landscape and, in turn, the product development approach. Going forward, the self-organized organizations that focus and organize around the customer are going to outperform their competition.

Chapter 4

Brainstorm and break down to breakthrough

As we know that software engineering and product development is a VUCA world, complex problems and challenges are an integral part of its journey. Changes are also inevitable in any project. Alterations might also be induced due to unclear scope or lacking requirements. Proactive steps should be taken to minimize the impact of the change on the project deliverables and timelines. The project manager does the risk assessment at regular intervals at each stage of the development, but there are still unknowns that can strike anytime.

Some of the scenarios when you encounter an issue or a roadblock are, for example,

- You are halfway through in your product development when the team realizes that the design put up has some technical limitations in terms of developing it with the technology stack that is in current use. The team has hit the roadblock, leaving them primarily with two options, change the technology stack or change the architecture/design.

- You, as an engineering manager, is assigned a complex program that is due to meet the tight and aggressive timelines.

The program is novel for the team and lacks expertise and skillset to work on it. There are also no experts available in the domain and technology within the organization who can be onboarded, to help the team with the strategy and plan.

- The customers have raised a production bug, and on initial analysis, it does not seem to have a straightforward fix. The defect identified in the core functionality of the product, and hence the repair may have impact and ramifications to the other components & flows in the product suite. The pressure is mounted from the customers for the fix at the earliest as the defect is impacting their business and revenue. They are also levying penalties on your company due to this issue.

These are some of the few everyday situations that we come across. I, too, have landed in such cases many times, especially when you least expect them to happen. The evident and instant reaction to such conditions is panic and pressure contemplating how and where to start. Whom to approach for guidance and what to do to solve the case, are the questions running in your mind. You are more uncertain than anybody as you have no clue about the solution and the steps to solve it.

I have been through this experience multiple times, but the one that I vividly remember was the one when I was working with a product development company. I was asked to manage a complex program for which the development manager had resigned from the company. The program was already delayed and was overrunning on budget and schedule. The business was impacted as they were unable to improve efficiency in their customer service process and operations due to this delay in the program. There was also a list of other initiatives across the company that were on hold due to this program. The strategic program had the visibility to the topmost brass of the company, and the CEO's office was tracking it daily.

For the first few weeks, I chose to just observe silently on how the work transpires in the team. The then development manager, who was about to leave the organization, provided knowledge about the product, groups, and stakeholders. He briefed me on the program objective and the consumers/users of the product that was in development.

I started to observe the critical pieces of the engineering followed for the product development. To begin with, the channel through which the work/requirement flows from product owner to engineering teams. The level of details & depth of the laid out requirements, captured in the user stories with clear acceptance criteria and targeted users, by the product team. The amount of time that is devoted to groom a story, architect & design the feature, reviews, estimation, and developing the story. When I was briefed about the continuous program delay, terrible product quality, and customer discontent, it was clear and evident that something was not right at the fundamental level of software engineering. The teams were not following the engineering best practices for some reason, resulting in a toiling day in and day out. Also, the results were not showing irrespective of their hard work and arduous efforts. The sincerity and dedication of the team was tremendous. Still, there was something not followed due to which the output was delayed, with a faulty product, adding no value to the customers. Instead, the customers were complaining, frustrated and annoyed.

There were two main points I noticed primarily from my one month (two sprint) observation. Firstly, the team was bombarded with too many unplanned and random tasks during their sprint cycle. These tasks were not necessarily related to the main program but peripheral support tasks or minor enhancements that the internal business team demanded. Such tasks were pushed to the team on priority, forcing them to put aside their planned jobs for that sprint. It would falter the entire sprint plan due to a lack of time, focus, and spillovers. The second thing was the stories and tasks given to the engineering team by the product management were of inferior quality. The stories were written at a very high level without any detailed description and the use case. The acceptance criteria were missing in most of the stories. The epic was not thought through and set out clearly from end to end business requirement perspective, due to which the subsequent stories and sub-tasks within that epic were disjointed and inadequate.

The engineering team was expected to pick up these unbaked requirements and build them. The issue that was typically faced by the team was rework and rework. They would develop it with their understanding based on the skewed and distorted information provided to them. And later, during the demo, the product owner would either add a new requirement on the fly or would conveniently mark it incomplete as it did not meet his expectations. The teams, including product management, lacked the real understanding of agile or somewhat misunderstood it to bespoke the entire methodology to suit their convenience.

As a result, the outcome was a failure. Everyone was in a mad rush, the product management to give twisted, unplanned work to the engineering team, and they would, in turn, be in a hurry to develop and deliver it. In a nutshell, discipline, deliberation, and dividing the requirements/work into smaller components were completely missing. Lack of granularity and lucidity on the task posed a continual challenge to the team, resulting in wastage of their energy & effort in unproductive activities.

The best technique to start in such a random and unpredictable environment is to do mind maps.

A mind map is a visual way to represent thoughts, ideas, or solutions. It is a proven framework that helps to bring out the thought clutter from mind to a piece of paper/whiteboard. It is a tool to structure your information and ideas in such a way that it can be better analyzed, linked, and knit easily. It is effortless to learn this technique. You leverage mind-mapping techniques in several ranges like product ideation, conceptualization, requirement gathering & prioritization, or determining the value proposition of the product. It proves handy when you recognize fix for a thorny problem, design solutions for a feature, classify test cases for a production rollout, or entire planning of the program from scratch. In a mind map, the information is structured in a way that resembles the working of your brain. The main topic or the subject in mind is in the center of the map. From the center, the related ideas and keywords will branch out in all directions. It results in a radiant type structure.

I learned and tried this method for the first time in my engineering days. It proved to be a fantastic learning tool to take my notes from the lectures, revise and memorize the important points during the exam preparation. Colors added magic to the mind map. Using different colors helped me to recollect the event prompts and connections. The hierarchy and relationships became very easy to recall, which was otherwise extremely difficult through linear thinking and reading traditional text. I never felt strenuous, or exhaustive, during the process. Instead, it was fascinating and fun doing it.

Knowing its benefits and value, I continued using the mind mapping technique in my software development journey. Initially, I used it to plan my coding and associated tasks/checks to perform. Later on, I started using it primarily in the design and planning phase of the software development. It provides extreme clarity to all those who participate in the mind mapping exercise, post which it helps all of us to work in alignment with a clear roadmap, strategy, and goal. The best part of this technique is that the colleagues, who are generally quiet and not that vocal to share their thoughts and suggestions, are also active participants in this process.

It provides everyone with a platform to contribute their views and ideas in a much open way, without any apprehension. It makes the mind mapping exercise more meaningful and more abundant in terms of objective and output. I witnessed more collaboration and communication between the team members during the mind-mapping exercise. Remote team members were also able to add their points/views, as the visual diagram, branching, and connections provided them immediate understanding.

Drawing a mind map is very easy. Following steps should be followed to create one -

1. *Set the whiteboard or the blank white page in a landscape orientation. The page should be completely blank without any lines. Then, write or draw the central idea that you intend to develop in the middle of a whiteboard/ blank page.*

2. *Develop the related subtopics and points around the central topic, connecting each of them to the center with lines or branches.*

3. *Repeat the same process for these subtopics, generating lower-level subtopics and connecting them to the corresponding subtopic with the sub-branches. You can also show dependency or any sort of linkage between two topics or subtopics by connecting them with dotted lines.*

Few points to remember while generating mind maps, to make it more useful and engaging,

- *Be creative and use more visuals. Our brain prefers visuals over text. Visuals are more impactful, easy to remember and recall.*

- *Use colors and other visual cues like text size, branch thickness, etc. to highlight and emphasize important points and relationships.*

- *Label the topics and branches, preferably in not more than one or two words. You should refrain from writing texts and long sentences.*

- *Use right mind mapping tools like XMind, Mindmup, etc., available on-premise or on the web to have active brainstorming sessions with distributed teams. These tools can translate the nodes into high-level milestones and project schedules.*

Brainstorm

My next goal was to start implementing this technique with my team first. We got into a conference room, along with colored marker pens. We invited the product owner for the session, and we locked ourselves in that room for two hours. I created a cloud-form at the center of the whiteboard with the product name in it. Then we forked out multiple branches from that center into goals that were intended to be achieved through the product. Each subtopic represented one goal in terms of one customer problem or the business outcome. These goals were at a high-level, for example, faster time to market by three months, cost reduction by 15%, automated incident creation, redirection, and many more.

Each of these goals/subtopics branched out further into multiple product features and functionalities that would allow us to achieve that goal. Then, we broke the features further into smaller branches and nodes that would represent components. These components would help to make that functionality. We tagged a few of these components as 'N' that expressed 'New features' as these would have to be developed from the scratch. The remaining parts highlighted in the mind map were existing ones that had to be either enhanced or used as it is. In this way, we kept breaking it into smaller and smaller pieces until that point that it could not split anymore.

Break down

The product owner helped us in terms of validating the requirements and the usage of the components. We also drew linkages between the nodes that had dependencies, explicitly calling out the teams who own that specific component with different color marker pens. We dedicated a particular color to highlight one goal and all its child nodes and branches so that it becomes easy to understand and interpret. This exercise provided an approximation in terms of the total work, efforts, and time at a high level to my team and product management. We tried our best not to deviate from the objective of this mind-mapping exercise and refrained from discussing the technical feasibility and implementation part. The complete session took more time than we anticipated, but that was worth it, as there was a sense of satisfaction, confidence, and more alignment on the requirements and features to develop in the product. It was the first work break down exercise, in a real sense that the team performed together to achieve common goals.

Work break down - in simple words, is the process to break down work into the smallest piece to be developed and managed. It is a recommended practice that each chunk of work does not take more than ten days or one sprint to build. Another rule applied is 8/80, while breaking the work into smaller pieces. It implies that no task should be more minor than eight hours of work and should not be larger than eighty hours of work.

Duplicacy should be avoided while determining these work chunks. If the same piece of work is required at multiple places, then a simple reusable piece should be built instead of cloning and patching it at various places in the code. During the mind mapping exercise, the requirements broke down from the highest to the nth level. The participants realized the importance and benefit of the mind mapping technique through which they witnessed cross-pollination of ideas and thoughts among themselves. They were also able to tie knots and establish a relationship in their points and suggestions in a visual form. The most important part was the enjoyment and fun they had during this entire exercise.

Imagine, the team doing the requirement gathering and understanding for the product by going through a 100-pager document filled with tedious text and verbose, on their own without any discussion or cross-collaboration. It would be a dreadful, time-consuming route for the engineers without any clarity and comprehension in the end.

Post the mind mapping exercise, the team utilized the information from the session, and improvised it further. The map was translated into a more structured format to be shared with architects for their review. The team created a table for each split component that had the dependencies, infrastructure requirements, technology requirements, contract mapping, mode of handshake, frequency of usage, and vital non-functional requirements applicable for that specific component. It was how the team put together the requirements and design at a high level for the product. The design was then shared with the architects for their review.

Meanwhile, the team delved into the next level of brainstorming to identify and spot those components that can be made generic and reusable across other functionality and the flows within the product. The intent was to develop these components in a very generic form so that they are applied at multiple places with just a customized wrapper on top of it.

The team thought through to leverage the concept of assembly line development used in factories, which is the norm in the manufacturing and automobile industries. The different parts/modules are built-in different independent zones, which are assembled in one standard line by attaching and bringing them together. The aim was to create a library or an asset pool of key reusable components that can be picked up and applied in the product suite offered by the company. A good amount of time was spent on the concept, specifications, and design part as the fundamentals of the product should be reliable and scalable in such a way that it can serve the customers for some years down the line.

Some intermediate enhancement and customization may be required from time to time, but the basic design and chassis of the product should remain intact. The more brainstorming and deliberation on the concept and design, the more it becomes easy to develop and integrate. Most of the queries w.r.t. Implementation was mull over from all angles in the sessions, facilitating faster development. The development also becomes less prone to errors in terms of functional testing at the component and integration level.

The next step was to work on the low-level design. This part can be done in parallel to avoid wastage of time. The team was logically (based on the components) broken down in pairs based on the expertise and experience. Out of two, one would have more experience compared to the other one. Each pair was assigned one component and ownership to work on the low-level design, get it reviewed by the technical leads, architects, and build it ultimately. Enough time should be allocated to all independent pairs to come up with the low-level design of their respective component and document it.

It was their responsibility to interact, collaborate with other team members, if required, and get the dependency worked out, which is necessary for the end-to-end working of the use case and the component flow. The review mechanism was put in place so that technical leads and architects evaluate the design. It helped them to focus entirely on their component. It also provided an opportunity to communicate with other pairs to ensure that the interaction between their components are developed in parallel and tested in an integrated way. The teammates would reach out to the technical leads, in case of any queries or huddles that they would face in building their respective component. The team made it from scratch with the ownership and accountability in their circle of influence for their segment.

Order of Creation

The requirement, features, and components were broken down in the smallest parts to the extent to develop independently and in parallel. However, the development sequence still needs to be planned; the component size in terms of complexity, effort, order, and time to establish were different. Few components depend on each other in terms of integration, and hence the determining and planning the development chain is also crucial. The idea was first to develop those components that have a dependency and will be required by other parts to test their functionality. The independent components, with no immediate reliance on others, should be built in parallel. The testing colleagues should not be blocked due to the unavailability of the module at any point. These components are identified and prioritized to create.

Based on the effort and complexity, a tentative schedule and plan was put up. This plan provided clarity to the team on the upcoming milestones, by when the components will be ready so that they can plan their next steps and proceed accordingly. The sequencing optimizes the time and minimizes the risk of any errors/surprise at the later stage of the product development.

Sequencing is a necessary step in product development. Most of the time, this step is missed by the engineering team in a rush to commence their development work. The repercussions crop up later in terms of rework, cost overrun, and timeline delays. The sequencing also helps to identify the integration points and handshake between the components. It might completely miss and overlooked if the order of creation is not followed. The team may develop a part and get it ready only to realize that it cannot be tested, as the dependent component is not yet prepared. Mutually exclusive elements that are independent in their functioning does not require dependency and sequencing. They can be developed and tested in a silo, in parallel.

Sequencing exercise also provides clarity to other teams in the environment who may be responsible for developing downstream/upstream modules in the product. They can accordingly plan their sprint and work to make those components available to you. The order of forming the elements should be highlighted in the plan, preferably visually for everyone to understand and have a clear picture. Sequencing enables the team in rapidly emerging and prototyping with the focus on the critical paths, structuring the user flows that matter to customers and business.

There are multiple software tools available to create the work break down and linkages. MPP (Microsoft Project Planner) is a potent tool to develop the entire program and project plan with a bottom-up or a top-down approach. The MPP can be used to plan projects irrespective of the development methodology (agile, iterative, waterfall, etc.) that is adopted by the team. JIRA is also widely used by product development companies to plan their sprint and release work. The product backlog is easy to maintain in JIRA, and that is the reason it becomes a prominent platform to do the sprint grooming, planning, and retrospective. These tools are equipped with Gantt charts for sequencing, dependency branching, widgets and dashboards for monitoring the progress and reporting. Microsoft Excel can also be beneficial for the entire product development lifecycle if your company is a start-up and does not want to invest money in these expensive tools & platforms.

Effort estimation, budgeting, time tracking, and costing are some of the other vital add-ons in these tools and platforms. It makes it easier for the manager to track cost and effort metrics as well, along with the schedule and quality. Resource planning and allocation will also be optimum, post the breakdown, and sequencing is carved out. The resources, their skillsets, and expertise can be ramped up & down, based on the development phase and the components that are in the making. It avoids the concentration and wastage of effort of all critical resources on the same module, and preferably they can be utilized in a better way if allocated across multiple components in parallel.

Breakthrough

Once the design, break-up and the plan for the development are in place, the construction itself became quite smooth and easy. The product owner was clear on the epics and stories to be created, as per the prioritized requirements. The engineering team knew the technical tasks to be created for those business stories and needs. The sprint ceremonies for each sprint, especially the story grooming, planning, and retrospectives, became shorter and effective. The demos became more fruitful to product owners and volunteer customers. The feedback cycle of seeking, prioritizing, and incorporating it in the product sped up. The meetings on the calendar of every team member reduced significantly. It helped the scrum team to self-organize and achieve better velocity and productivity. The team spent quality time in building the features. They were not driving to meet the MVP (Minimum Viable Product) requirements; instead, they were relentless in coming up with a MAP (Minimum Amazing Product). The team dynamics changed utterly.

Three months back, the engineering team was clueless and fatigued, working for crazy hours, applying their effort and time on unplanned tasks. That transformed. They are now smartly working for 8 hours a day, with a clear focus and relentless drive to meet the goal of developing a cool product for the customers. It brought in satisfaction, content, and a sense of achievement during their software building voyage.

Components were built and stitched together, ultimately shaping up in a product. The system integration, performance, end-to-end, and user acceptance testing was completed successfully. The product was released successfully. The customers loved the product, and to our astonishment, the adoption numbers were an all-time high. It was a breakthrough, primarily in terms of the performance of the product. The user flows were amazingly fast, satisfying the needs of the customers.

The breakthrough may attain in new or existing products of the company, but with a considerable improvement, in terms of performance, user experience, or in the form of technology leap. Sony launched its first iconic portable cassette player Walkman back in July 1979. Around 400 million Walkman were sold across the globe. It was a breakthrough in terms of listening to music whenever and wherever you want. There was a paradigm shift in the music industry, in the way music was stored, sold, and consumed. Netflix disrupted the movie market by shortening the time to deliver movies and eventually streaming it online.

The point I am trying to make is that you can build amazing products, if the focus and enough time is invested in the concept and design phase, followed by breaking down into smaller buildable chunks and striking the right chord with your targeted customers. You can choose to build something just to meet requirements, or you can choose to create a state of the art product that makes your customers say, WOW!.

The work break down approach is typically used by project managers to define and organize the project work. But this practical approach should be promoted and extended in all stages of software development. In the example mentioned above, the team used it first to break down the requirements, and further to break down the work is stories and tasks. It not only helped to manage the work by team members but also in identifying dependencies and risks.

The progress report on the feature development is more appropriate and meaningful if they are tracked at the component level. All the individual workpieces should be able to connect in a branch or a path. The ones which are loosely held or have no connection are the areas which have risk. It also helps the team to impact assess the delay in project milestones and identify the component in the whole path, causing the snag. Once it is determined, the team can have a reasonable mitigation plan and focus on that troubled component.

The brainstorming and break down approach not only provides breakthroughs in the product but also in other aspects of software engineering. The teams achieve productivity breakthroughs as they are now able to develop and turnaround the new component and functionality at a much faster rate than before. A lot of the confusion, questions, and concerns are addressed at the initial stage itself, which is why teams can pace well in creating the product.

The integration plan and upfront dependency identification avoid shockers and unknowns to a great extent on their path. The productivity of the team is pivotal to the success of the product. It can hamper the strategic goal of the company if the team is low on this parameter. The direct implication is on the cost of the product as it will increase, if the productivity is low, eventually hitting the profitability numbers. It will also significantly delay the time to market due to which the company will lose the customers, market share, and revenue.

Quality is paramount in any product as it directly determines the customer experience. Low quality can not only fail the product but also put the company out of business. Moreover, the reputation of the company and brand equity is also lost, making it extremely difficult for them to sustain in the future. The consequences of it can be grave. A financial institution or a bank can lose millions of dollars due to a software bug, while a credit union company can lose confidential customer data to the hackers. It can make medical equipment manufacturer and the automobile maker to recall their goods. A software glitch can result in a divorce when a ride-hailing app started popping up notifications in the logged-out state on the wife's phone, revealing his husband's travel and destination history details.

Software bugs in the past, and continues to cost lives, businesses, reputation, and spark chaos. With the brainstorming and the break down approach at the requirement and design stage itself, the chances of inducing defects during the development becomes feeble. It helps prevent the work from slipping through the cracks. It also reduces the rework considerably for the teams. Software bugs prove to be costlier, if identified at the later stages of the product development and deployment.

Quality should remain un-compromised at any stage. It should be monitored actively at every stage/milestone with a strict passing criterion. Complex defects and bugs should be deliberated first within the team to explore possible options to fix it. An optimal and practical solution should be identified and applied to correct the problem. Our minds will get restricted/biased in thinking when we are working on a high-pressure task or a defect. Brainstorming it with the team and more minds relives the pressure and enables us to think in a better and broader way.

The engineering manager should ensure that the team can focus on the right solution and conceal them from all the noise & stress that the management, stakeholders apply at that point. The testing cycle and time planned at the start of the project should not be shortened to meet the timelines. The quality assurance team should be empowered with all the freedom and bandwidth to exhaustively test the functionality before it is marked as ready for release to the customers. It will help engineering teams to thoroughly examine the product before it goes into the hands of the users. Customer adoption can increase leaps and bounds due to good quality and a comforting user experience.

The WBS (Work Break down Structure) approach provides visibility to the management in terms of the complexity, amount, and efforts that are required to build a system. In the end, once the project concludes, and the product is ready, the team should retrospect on the efficacy of the break down exercise done at the start. There will be areas of improvement that should be noted and ensured that it is taken care of in the next assignment. Brainstorming, break down, and establishing the order to build form the fundamentals for the success of any product/project that can smoothen the entire concept to the market journey. Engineering teams should adopt this style, not only at the start, but at all stages and junctures of the project. They should embed it as a critical and mandatory step to follow.

The team, especially the engineering manager, should not lose sight of the work break down and the traceability created at the start of the project. He should take the ownership to regularly groom, alter and evolve it at a regular frequency in consultation with the team. The progress monitoring and reporting should consolidate at each component level. It brings in more accuracy and credibility to the reports. The engineering manager or the lead should facilitate brainstorming sessions for even the smallest piece of work so that the team comes up with the best possible solution. These things bring the team together, builds trust, and fosters a cohesive culture. The colleagues in the team not only feels positive and valued, but also accomplished. It brings in the sense of ownership and better decision making amongst the colleagues. You cannot bring a transformational change or build great products unless you decompose and understand the problem to its core.

'Breakthroughs can come from break down or breakdowns.'

Chapter 5

Who is Who in the Zoo?

Stakeholders! You must be well conversant with this word if you are part of the software IT industry. This term, most of the time, is used loosely for just referring to senior management of the company. Sometimes, it is used as a mechanism to create pressure on the team by the manager. You must have come across your manager stating that the stakeholders will be unhappy if a particular task does not finish on time.

Well, stakeholders are much more than that. In simple words, they have a stake or an interest in the project/program that the team is working on. Stakeholders can be internal or external to the organization. Internal ones work within and are from the same organization, and the external ones are outside the organization, but they have an interest in the project. They are going to be directly or indirectly impacted by the results and outcome of the program. Customers are also part of the stakeholders, investors as well. The developer and the tester is also a stakeholder. An engineering leader or a manager is a stakeholder too. Teams on which you are dependent on something are also your stakeholders. They all are in different positions, playing varied roles and responsibilities. And that is the reason, and their stakes are also different in the program. Customers are interested in the functionality of the product and how it is going to solve their problems. An investor is concerned about the profitability of post product sales. The seamless working of the product is what matters to the developer and tester. And for an engineering manager, it is to deliver the product within the estimated budget and timelines. Everyone has a different purpose, need, and ways to look into the same program.

Stakeholder management is a vital piece in any program and project execution. It is the process of maintaining good and healthy relationships with them, as they are the ones who are getting impacted by your work, project, and program. Stakeholder management is a crucial ingredient for a successful project. But many times, we consider it as a peripheral activity without giving due consideration and importance to it. Typically, the project or the program manager is responsible for performing stakeholder management activities. However, in the product development world, this lies more with the engineering manager. It is not easy as it may seem to be because wherever there are people, there are challenges to manage their expectations, their working style, and to align with their thought process. It can be overwhelming and grueling at times to deal with a few of them, especially when they are anxious, upset, uncertain, or irritated about something. They may react unexpectedly during the phases of the project, when challenges and issues are causing a risk to the timelines and completion of the project. That is the time when most of them will react in the traditional 'fight-or-flight' mode.

The term 'fight-or-flight' represents the choice that an individual takes when there a problematic situation arises. At that time, the individual will either choose to fight or flee. In the software development world, the uncertain situation could be a risk to the project completion, issues faced by customers post product release, or any unexpected and unprecedented situation. In such difficult circumstances, there will be only a few stakeholders who will understand the program situation, the challenges it is facing, and accordingly contribute and add value for the success of it. They will provide direction to the team based on their wisdom and experience. They may also take charge and bring alignment with other stakeholders in terms of the situation and the mitigation steps.

The best and the recommended step before you start on any project or the program is to develop a stakeholder management strategy. Devising a strategy to manage your stakeholders is equally important as it is to create an execution plan for the program or the technical design for a product. The tactic will depend on multiple factors - the complexity, size, and duration of the program. A more extensive program with enormous business impact, a high budget, and for a longer-term qualifies for a stakeholder management strategy.

The next step is to identify the stakeholders associated with the program. You should come up with a complete list of the names of the stakeholders, their role with influence, and the expectation they have from the program. In such programs, especially, the stakeholders play a crucial role in providing sponsorship, guidance, and reviews. They will also be the decision-maker in terms of giving a go/no-go ahead to the production release. They will be the ones who will approve your estimated effort, budget, and team size. They can also provide support and recommend interim need to procure specific tools or vendors to expedite the program execution. There will be a constant inflow of their inputs and decisions that needs to be tracked and communicated effectively. Hence, the need for a good stakeholder communication plan is a must. In the communication plan, you should lay out the reporting channel, format, metrics, cadence, weekly program review with them, and the channel to share risks, mitigation, decisions, program artifacts.

Stakeholders play a valuable role in the success and failure of any program. Identifying the right set of stakeholders is the key, if not done at the inception of the program itself. There are multiple frameworks and ways in which stakeholders can be identified and classified. The most used ones are to list all the stakeholders and then map them in a 2 x 2 quadrant of Interest vs. Power or the RASCI matrix. In Interest vs. Power, there are four quadrants in terms of high-interest, low-power, high-interest high-power, low-interest low-power, and low-interest low power. Every quadrant will give you a corresponding response and management technique for these stakeholders based on their interests and power levels. In the RASCI matrix approach, stakeholders are bucketed in five categories which are Responsible, Accountable, Supportive, Consulted, and Informed. These categories are based on their focus, role, and level of involvement in the program. Based on the bucket, a management and communication strategy is sketched out for that set of stakeholders.

The challenge in these approaches is that it is not only time consuming but also gets difficult to conclude on the understanding of the power and interest of all stakeholders. In the RASCI approach, the stakeholder might keep shifting within the buckets during the program execution based on their change in interests. You come to know about these parameters gradually as you work more with them. You should know at a high level on who are your important ones and then keep evaluating them in due course of the program. You also need to keep your RASCI list updated based on the movements of the role in the stakeholders. These two approaches bring in a lot of overhead for the manager to maintain and keep the stakeholder list updated. A lot of the manager's time and effort is wasted in these practices.

The below approach that I have elaborated has worked well for me as it is simpler and not much time-consuming. As an engineering leader, you should spend more time on building the product to solve customer problems. That is what matters for the growth of my company. You should spend more time with your team on the product development. The brainstorming on multiple approaches to solve a problem, discussions on how to remove the impediments for the team, automate recurring steps of a process, ideate and innovate on new functionality, improve quality, and customer experience are the areas on which you should be focusing more. Because in the end, the results matter. The stakeholders will automatically align and will be happy if the business outcomes are accomplished.

Most of the time, handling the stakeholder community depends on how well you understand the internal company dynamics and political affairs. It seems to be simple but can be complicated and tricky to manage. I am, personally, not inclined to spend my extra time or the effort in such things. That is the reason why I always take this relatively simple and, to some extent, a fun approach to manage my stakeholders. So to start, I create a list of all stakeholders associated with the program and classify them in two broad categories, one who is genuinely interested in the success of the program and can add constructive value to the team.

In contrast, the other set comprises of the ones, who will merely add no or nuisance value to the program. As a program or the development manager, my focus is always on the first category and perform bare minimum activities for the other set. The thumb rule is again the success of the program, and hence investment of your time and effort should always be in those stakeholders who can help you achieve it. It is not worth and not going to bear any fruitful results if that momentum is directed for the second set of stakeholders as they will digress your focus and impact the pace and outcome of the project.

Now the next obvious question would be on how we can classify the stakeholders. The rule is to sort based on their role, working style, behavior, and impact. You need to be sensitive in this zone as you are dealing with humans, and they are all different. The response and reaction to a particular situation will differ from stakeholder to stakeholder.

Here is how we can do it. First things first, you need to invest a reasonable amount of time in observing and analyzing every stakeholder's behavior linked with your product/program, especially with the ones that you will be dealing with in all your interactions, meetings, and discussions. Try to understand their style of working, characteristics, and expectations. You can have one-on-one talks planned with each stakeholder to understand their views and hope from the program. You should do this exercise with only those stakeholders with whom you are going to work with directly.

Initial one-on-one conversations help to break the ice and create a comfortable space between you and the stakeholder. You can manage your stakeholders effectively only if you understand the intricacies of their behavior, nature, position, and the responsibility that they possess. And that can be done only with more interactions. It is straightforward in smaller or short-duration projects. However, it becomes very complex and challenging when it is an extensive program and a more prolonged running assignment. The stakeholder management can eat up most of your time if not done in a structured and systematic way.

I continue to learn from my experience in this space where I deal with different types of roles. They could be the sponsors, CXOs, senior leadership, board members, customers, mid-level managers, cross-team members, architects, business analysts, vendors, teammates, etc. Managing stakeholders for a few of the programs which I did, was challenging and an immense learning experience on how to manage them better. It is with the time you learn to work and deal with them. You cannot handpick your stakeholders; they come along with the assignment or program. It is like relatives where you do not have the choice to select the way we do with our friends. Dealing with friends is a lot easier than dealing with your relatives. But you must survive and maintain a good relationship with them, as they are part of the family. Similar is the case with stakeholders; you do not have the liberty to opt-out and say that you do not want to work with an individual stakeholder. Instead, you need to work out a healthy relationship with them and strive until you accomplish it.

Some stakeholders are too sensitive, and for them, small & minor issues can also spark the 'fight or flee' mode. They can be paranoid and cause more noise unnecessarily due to their nature, behavior, or some sense of insecurity. As a result, you will end up spending most of your time to address that person's concern, pressure, or any difference of opinion, if there is any. These stakeholders will tend to cage you in their influence, expecting data & status as per their need and stress you with some random ad-hoc tasks. They can become overwhelming and frustrating for you to manage them, impacting yours, and the overall program schedule.

Based on my learnings, there are typically four types of stakeholders based on their role, behavior, expectation, and the style of working. The toughest part is to identify these traits and classify them in the following categories that I have written about below. Once you identify the type of stakeholder, working with them becomes much more structured and more comfortable. It also helps to keep the relationship sound and healthy. The initial phase of establishing the type of stakeholder may be time-consuming, but it becomes straightforward later on.

The Oblivious Pandas

Pandas are well-known for their stumbling and languid nature. They sleep for around ten hours a day, and will doze pretty much anywhere. They devote their time to eating when they are awake. They are solitary animals by nature, and they avoid contacting with others. They are one of the lethargic animals on the planet. Research shows that pandas use only 38% of their energy that an animal with the same body mass would require. Pandas are generally docile but can be aggressive if they are irritated and disturbed from their comfort zone. They are calm and peace-loving animals. They love to spend most time sleeping/dreaming on a tree without being concerned about what is transpiring around.

Stakeholders with panda personalities are not interested in the project or the program. They are not willingly part of the project, and hence they do not care about what is going in it. Due to their silence and no participation in the discussions or meetings, you will sometimes not realize their presence as well. They are unaware of the context, objective, or the roadmap of the entire program. They are clueless about the project operations. They are merely present just for the sake of it. They add no value, but at the same time, they will also not cause any trouble to you. They will not add noise or provide any unnecessary inputs in the reviews and meetings. They are merely doing their nine-to-five job who are particular for their in-time, lunch, tea, and out-time. They are comfortable in their world, work routine, and are entirely sorted with it.

You can choose to ignore these stakeholders. Their presence or absence does not matter or impact your project in any way. You should not spend time collecting data, making reports, or providing status to this set of stakeholders as they are not interested. They are passive listeners, which means that they may seem to be listening and understanding, but it is far from reality. You should let them enjoy their zone and do not probe or instigate them for anything. Do not waste your time in seeking any help or direction from them, as it is going to be of no use. In short, these stakeholders are more content if they are not involved or pulled in any project deliberations. You need to ensure they are part of all decisions and status updates. There are high chances that they may not even have a glance at it, but they need to be an intrinsic part of all the stakeholder messaging.

The Flashy Peacocks

The peacock is sexy and beautiful. They love to be the center of attention and crave for constant praise and reassurance. Most of the peacock's time is spent on improving tactics to enhance its status. They are incredibly obsessive about themselves. Peacocks are an attention-seeker who enjoys nothing more than showing off. Peacocks like to show their vivacious colors, their feathers and highlight their beauty. These elegant natural birds are most suited for professions like wedding planning, interior designing, or structural architects. They are a complete misfit in the software industry. They would not understand what is occurring in the project and have no hint about the details; however, they know how to claim their dwindling patina by highlighting themselves in a forum or a high stakeholder discussion.

The stakeholders who have these characteristics are part of the program merely to show their presence. They will highlight their presence in a gathering or dialogue by asking some irrelevant questions or by making a trivial point. The intent is just to highlight the presence and inform everyone that 'I am there.' They will reveal off as if they know everything about the project and will provide their unsolicited opinions randomly, but that does not mean anything. They will not own or take accountability for any task, but they would not leave a single opportunity to hold others accountable and delegate, especially in group conversations or consultations. They will hear some words here & there and will randomly sprinkle them out in some other meetings and discussions. They are adept at creating confusion with their inadequate knowledge of the project.

You cannot completely ignore them as they are part of your stakeholder list. You need to realize how to handle this type of personality. Acknowledge their point whenever they make and move on. Do not bother to give it a thought or any time to discuss it further. They will never follow-up with you or come back on that point again that they had brought up in the conversation. Do not spend your time in mining information and providing data to them as they are least interested. Keep them in loop upfront in all the decisions and reports that you generate, and you can ignore the points that they make, especially in the more prominent forums.

The alternate way to handle such a personality is to assign them an action item in a meeting and follow-up proactively with them at the start of the next session. You should ask their views on a critical issue or on a challenging problem that you are facing in the project. Put them on the spot to seek their ideas. Initially, they would babble something but eventually will get low progressively in terms of showing off. A little bit of aggressiveness and proactiveness can put these stakeholders on the back foot, allowing you to focus on your program and the stakeholders that matter, adds value to the project.

The Pouncing Panthers

Black panthers are unique cats in their family with the ability to roar. They are mainly evasive and are scarce in number. They generally like to be in stealth mode and are rightly called as the ghost of the forest. A panther would typically climb a tree with an incredible ease or be on top at a certain height and would wait for long to identify its prey and pounce on it in a fraction of a millisecond. They do not hunt in herds but prefer to hunt alone.

Stakeholders with these characteristics are merely there to roar and pounce on you. They will try to catch a mistake, gap, or some insignificant issue in the execution and create a big fuss around it.

They will scream, growl, and will try to hurt/impact the implementation by creating unnecessary noise. They are dangerous and can influence the decision-makers by painting the wrong picture by continuously harping on it. They choose to be vocal on an issue/problem rather than providing solutions or mitigation to it. They can get down the morale of the entire team. They are incredibly skilled in blaming others and the team when the cause of the issue is something else. They can turn around the tables quickly without even giving you a hint. They may seem to be sometimes supporting you in a conversation but eventually will come hard on you. You need to extra cautious from such stakeholders.

Being calm and having your due diligence done is the key to manage these types of stakeholders effectively. You must be vigilant with such a personality. You should be thorough in your preparations before any meeting, especially while conversing with them. You should keep your calm and composure to the highest levels while dealing with such stakeholders. Try to understand and validate the point at the same instance itself when they make it so that you know the implicit intent and actionable step to be taken for it. Confirm your understanding with them, in case of any confusion. You should refrain from giving them any chance for them to weed out any mistakes or irregularities.

Proactive communication with such stakeholders is the key. Connect with them in person before the meetings where you need their support or decision in your favor. You should be more assertive at times and highlight the gap at their end as well, in your one-on-one dialogue with them. It is not wise and recommended to be on the back foot with such stakeholders all the time. They might start to take your team for granted and have unreal expectations and tasks dumped on you. With such personalities, you should learn the art of saying NO whenever required, without losing your composure and poise. You should always remember that the person who is quiet and arranged in a conflict or a prolonged argumentative situation will be heard more and builds more credibility.

Active communication, interaction, and sometimes, over-communication with such stakeholders is the key to have a prolonged & good relationship with them.

The Wise Owl

The owl epitomizes equanimity and level-headedness in the species of birds. Owl is a creature of high integrity and is widely recognized as a serene, wise observer of human society. Owl is always well-groomed; it is a noble individual with beautiful large eyes with eyeglasses signifying a well-informed creature. They have developed a reputation for intellect due to their calm and listening nature. They are an astute observer and employ their deeper impulses for the next steps and guidance. These night-time creatures spend most of their time in a quiet working ambiance and venture out alone only if there is a need. They are not at all boisterous, societal, or bouncy like some of the other creatures' dolphins. They are reasonably gifted with good posture & size, and they also keep themselves physically fit.

Owls promote peacefulness, think logically, and argue cogently. They rarely get into the altercation mode and shows no signs of physical battle. They do not desire for a long-term fight. But, they do not shy away from opposing if needed to settle any lingering argument. As an astute observer, owls are suited for senior positions. Their trustworthiness and credibility make them perfect for areas of responsibility, perhaps as leaders, or decision-makers. A diligent worker, an owl, takes its obligations seriously and performs its duties rightfully. They achieve high stances and triumph in whatever they do due to their sheer hard work and perseverance.

Owls are the wisest of them all. They are well-read, well-informed about anything they do, and especially on the assignment that they take up. Stakeholders with the characteristics of an owl believe in factual data and numbers. They have the attitude to provide rational and workable solutions to the problems. They are the ones who give useful insights into the zones which you must have missed out or dropped the ball in your pursuit to conclude the product development and program. They are keen observers and excellent listeners. They will listen to everyone and will ultimately come up with a final and right decision to benefit the program. They are impartial and are always with the mindset to solve the root cause of the problem rather than the problem itself. They have the ability and the expertise to go in the depth and weeds of the program, execution challenges, and understand things that are transpiring at the ground level. They are quick to assimilate the nook & corner of the project and foresee risks/issues, the ones not thought or anticipated by the project team. These proficiencies come to them from their rich knowledge and work experience.

The entire focus should be mainly on these stakeholders by the engineering leader and the manager. They will proactively provide timely support and suggestions that will not only add value to your program but also keep it on track. You should always be honest and transparent with them. You should provide them with the right data points and relevant information from time to time. It is ok to accept if you have messed up somewhere or have missed out anything. These personalities will always guide you through as a mentor. You should try and understand the perspective that they bring on the table, which provides a vibrant learning ecosystem not only to you but also to your colleagues and teammates.

You should build an alliance with such stakeholders and have regular one-on-one discussions with them to discuss and share your challenges, learnings, to seek their advice. And if you are fortunate, you may get a mentor in such a stakeholder that will groom your ability and potential in the broader career context and provide visibility for you. They act as the brand ambassador of the project and the program, wherein they will showcase the commendable work, and praiseworthy stuff achieved by the team, in the more prominent forums and presentations with senior brass and board.

The process of identifying the stakeholders' behavior and mapping it to a personality should be strictly for yourself. It should not be discussed or shared with anyone in the team or the company. It will only help you to strategize the communication and manage them effectively, ensuring the success of the entire program. The characteristics and behavioral mapping will be different for different people. It will be a more productive and helpful exercise based on how well you understand their traits. Once the stakeholder management strategy is formulated with the above steps, the implementation of the plan should start on the ground to handle them during the program journey.

Some more proven facets should be applied to have a persistent association with your stakeholders.

Collaborate and Communicate

The more you communicate with the stakeholders on your project, the more they feel valuable and engaged. You should keep sharing the critical information, status, and updates on the project with them at all stages. There should be nothing that should come to them as a surprise later. The reaction of stakeholders may vary and differ in different situations.

There is always a spark basis in which you may witness unexpected and abrupt reaction by the stakeholder. If you can identify these trigger points upfront, then these reactions can be mitigated or handled in a better way. For example, you have come across a critical issue in the final round of product testing just before the release. This bug may defer the release timelines. It will have a strong reaction from the stakeholders. It is true that not all the issues and risks can be predicted and foreseen until they occur. However, in this situation, your reporting update or earlier communication to the stakeholders should have explicit mention that the final round of testing is due before the release, and there are chances that unknown issues might surface, posing a risk to the timelines and schedule. In this way, the stakeholders would have known about this risk upfront rather than a surprise later. They might provide some suggestions to mitigate the risk if it was communicated to them earlier.

Proactive and over communication, at times, is recommended in certain stages of the project, especially when the team is in war-room or the final stages of the project when the nerves and pressure are high. The engineering manager/leader should be able to speak two languages at all times. He should be able to use the technical jargon to communicate with the teammates and the non-technical language with other stakeholders. He should act as a liaison between technical and non-technical stakeholders for information translation and exchange.

Common minimum program

This scenario will arise when different stakeholders have diverging requirements and priorities for the product. It will happen especially at the nascent phase of the project, where they would all need their demands to fulfill in the product, and on priority. That is the stage of the product and the program when you are not knowledgeable about the role, position, behavior, and influence of the stakeholders. It makes it tricky for the team to select the features/work and prioritize. In such situations, you should come up with the bare minimum feature list to develop in the product that will give the desired business outcome and value to customers in the shortest time. Post that, the remaining features should be discussed and pondered in due course with the right stakeholders and choose on the ones to be part of the minimum viable product and the remaining ones, to be developed and rolled out in subsequent production releases.

Be proactive in stressing potential risks and issues

Nobody likes undesired surprises, and that is the reason why you should be on your toes in doing a timely risk assessment of the program and share it with the stakeholders at a defined frequency. The stakeholders will appreciate when you highlight the anticipated risks and issues, but they will also be looking for the mitigation steps that you have planned. The steps should be clear, crisp, and well-articulated. They will not have time to go through the risk register or a laundry list of issues. They will be more interested in knowing the top three risks and problems that pose a threat to the next upcoming milestone and the overall program completion.

Document the decisions and rulings

The suggested practice, while dealing with stakeholders, is to keep the interaction and decisions in writing, either over emails, Confluence wiki pages, or any centralized knowledge repository of the project. There can be conversations over the phone, in person, or groups, but you should always capture and share the minutes of the meeting (MOM), and action items post the dialogue. In the software development journey, judgments are taken at every juncture. As humans, it is practically impossible to recall all of them and the basis they were made. They can cause conflicts later, and prove detrimental to the project if not documented at that very instance.

The crucial points from the consultations should be captured at a central project repository so that it can be fetched swiftly whenever required. It also helps new teams to take away and incorporate valuable lessons from the past executions when they plan the next product/functionality development or a new project. It accelerates their ability to design a similar project and eliminates their effort & time in reinventing the wheel. Prompt documentation drives expedited decision-making if an identical problem or situation is faced in the ensuing path.

Consult often with crucial stakeholders

You should have continual dialogues with your vital stakeholders (especially owls) at a regular frequency. You should seek advice and opinions on the explicit challenges that you witness. Most of the time, they will provide you the right direction, which you may have overlooked or not thought through. These exchanges also provide them assurance on the project-related stuff that is emerging at the ground level. It builds trust and credibility between the team and stakeholders, which is a prerequisite for an easy and smooth functioning of the project. They may also help in swaying other members and align them, if you are facing troubles in doing it yourself. The more you try and utilize their experience, the better it is for the team and the overall execution of the program.

Report crisp information and precise message

Information that you share with the stakeholders should be crisp and clear. Unstructured and too much information is difficult to absorb and retain in mind. You should know the precise message that you want to give it to stakeholders. The information & data should support and in alignment with the message.

It is a recommended practice to bullet your points instead of long textual paragraphs. You need to be sensitive and value the stakeholder's time and convey your information within that time. The attention span is limited, and hence long reports with too much verbose, text and slides are of no use. You should spend the least time in coming up with the report, and convey to-the-point data and inference. It will help the recipients to consume and absorb the points easily and quickly.

It is the area where most of the managers think; otherwise, they feel that they should provide as much information as possible to the stakeholders and the recipients. They will try to dump everything on them in a disorderly manner, but the intent and the purpose fails. That is the reason why, the stakeholders will end up being confused, uncertain about the data reported, and will either bombard you with too many questions or would not bother to ask any. The whole objective of informing and sharing essential insights goes for a toss, as it is lost somewhere in the data clutter. The manager's time is squandered in collating data and reports, with no meaning to the data consumers. Instead, you should have a crisp executive abstract on the top or at the start of the report that summarizes the entire gist of the project status. The executive summary should be followed by a few vital graphs, visuals and data points highlighting the trend and pattern of the execution.

Set a regular cadence for program reviews and reporting

Post the project planning is finished, and the onset of execution, you should set a recurring program reviews, and report dissemination protocol to communicate on the project status & progress to stakeholders. The cadence should be at least once every week. It can be extended to the fortnightly or monthly rate of recurrence to report aggregated data, logical milestones, and key accomplishments. It helps to keep them up to speed on the program condition.

 The program review should be collectively done in the presence of stakeholders and decision-makers. There should be delegates from engineering, product, QA, architects, vendors, sales, and marketing functions should be part of the review. The program manager should consolidate essential points, progress, and patterns to share it with the forum. The derived insights should be presented in a simple and consumable format to everyone.

The point-of-contacts from each function should raise their query or concern, if any, and seek solutions for it from the right stakeholder. A dedicated timeslot should be allotted to discuss the predicted risks and issues, to come up with suggestions & mitigation around it. The critical discussion notes, choices should be captured in the form of minutes at the end of the meeting and circulated as a record. The program review meeting should be time-boxed and driven through an agenda. There should be someone to facilitate the review session to keep it on track and avoid wastage of everybody's time. Otherwise, it can derail losing its need and purpose.

The program report's format and template are fundamental. You should design a simple, standard report layout, preferably in one slide or one page only, that covers the key metrics, dependencies, risks, mitigation, completed vs. upcoming milestones, and defect convergence. An executive summary in 3 – 5 bulleted points stemmed based on the trends, and the data should be included on the top. Visuals and graphs are preferred than plain text as images have a better brain-recall than the text.

An automated real-time reporting portal or a wiki page is also advantageous. Stakeholders can refer to that page and live feed anytime to get the real-time information and instantaneous status on the project. Different stakeholders will be interested in the varied details you provide. It is like reading a newspaper; some are interested in the sports news and some in politics. Some in astrology and some are interested in the crossword game.

Similarly, the stakeholders will look for different information. Quality bosses will be more interested in the defect injection and trend related data, while engineering chiefs will be looking for information in the number of features developed versus pending. Senior executives are focussed on the timeline and budget consumption. Therefore, setting a regular rhythm of providing all the relevant information to the stakeholders brings clarity, orientation, uniformity, reduces uncertainty and confusion in their minds. Above all, it saves your own time in delivering explanations and data to them on an ad-hoc / need basis.

Effective stakeholder management and healthy relationship sustenance can bring in business intelligence and insights basis, which you can derive new product ideas as well. You will learn from the stakeholders on what adds value to the customers and what does not. A relationship is never static. In more extensive and lengthy running programs, stakeholders will change, and so will their role, stakes, and expectations. Their level of interest might wax and wane depending on the stage and the state of the project.

Research shows that the project/engineering manager spends around 80% of its time in interactions and information exchange. It is not desirable at all. They should be spending more time on the product making, in resolving issues, challenges, and monitor it to be on course. A regulated and controlled approach in managing the stakeholders will help you to reap benefits for the project and avert anything to let fall between the cracks. It will also significantly reduce your interaction time with the stakeholders once the process is established and running smoothly. Appropriate identification of stakeholders, behavioral-role fitment, anticipating triggers at the right time, and expectation setting will not only reduce the risk and woes, but also propel you to take appropriate and timely measures to deliver a successful project ultimately.

Chapter 6

Fail fast to succeed faster with agile and discipline

There are always great ideas, and the companies/start-ups want to pursue that one idea, which they feel will make a difference in the market. But the idea is not substantial enough unless it gets the blessings from the market and the customers. You cannot determine the true potential and the market acceptance of the idea at the initial stage. The company should get that validated from the customers, at the concept stage itself, so that you can know if the path that they have embarked is in the right or the wrong direction. Validating your idea with the users becomes more inexorable when you have limited time and resources. It can save on both and avoid catastrophe later if the users do not find the idea useful.

In today's complex and continuously changing era of the product development market, there is not much time and liberty that the companies can avail in terms of predicting, researching, and building products at their own pace. They need to be extraordinarily fast in terms of bringing the products to the customers even before their competitors could do. You can also govern and measure anything predictable, but that is not the case in the software world, especially when it is changing at a mind-boggling rate. You cannot wait to build a perfect, solid product or a solution for the customers because that would take time. By the time you are ready with it, you will realize that the need and the problem of the customer have already changed or met by an alternate solution in the market that you were trying to solve.

The target should always be to build a decent enough product with minimalistic features, ship it quickly to the market, and continue to improve it based on the customer feedback. This approach helps you to gain from faster time to market and unceasingly enhance it with new functionalities, improvements through iterative learning from the users. Incremental learning also fosters a platform for the team members to adapt and mold themselves as per the customer needs. They inculcate more flexibility and agility gradually during the path, which would not have been the case otherwise.

The team members also get better and better in treating risks and doing shorter and quicker experiments. The continuous feedback loops for the prospective customers help them to understand the gaps in their philosophy and approach. It is always better to fail sooner and correct the course accordingly, than later, as it is significantly less costly in terms of efforts and dollars, if caught at the embryonic stage itself. That is the reason why the software or the product that you are building should be done iteratively in small components. These modules should be verified and validated through a constant feedback mechanism, integrated/discarded based on the collective decision, and then assembled to come up with the final complete product.

The process of developing small components iteratively and swiftly is the agile methodology. Agile methodology was introduced in 2001 as an alternative to other software development techniques like Waterfall, to achieve faster business outcomes with the help of flexibility, incremental development, and agility. It gives the company advantage in terms of taking their product to the market quickly and seek the pulse of the customers, before investing entirely on it.

There is also a lean way of development, which is like an agile process, with the same approach to build smaller pieces of the software, seek feedback and improve on it. It accelerates the learning, not only for the engineering teams but also for other functions within the company itself. In the VUCA world of the software market, you cannot remain disconnected from your customers at any point. You should be in constant touch with them through multiple channels to stay on the top of their needs and to be aware of the alternate solutions that are being provided by the competition.

The agile and lean ways of developing the software also provides a platform for the engineering teams to come up with innovative solutions in the product. It extends their thought process beyond the limits of the requirements laid out by the product management, that can add value and monetized by the company. The platform is also a testbed for them to test their ideas and innovations, capitalize on it if the customers accept them. Agile was perceived as an undisciplined way of working during its initial inception phase. But, today, it has become the de-facto way to construct the software in almost every company.

In the B2B (Business to Business) scenario, the customers from banks, financial institutions, e-commerce, retail, manufacturing, insurance, automobile, etc. sectors are also tying up deals with the IT product and service companies who have matured in the agile methodology. They want to continually observe the form of the product at intermediate phases and provide their inputs & feedback along the course to avoid any unwanted surprises later.

In the agile/lean journey, the co-location of the team is the primary pillar for it to be successful. The partnership between the team members should be super quick and continuous. Collaboration among them should be comfortable so that they can develop and test the component in parallel, without depending on much on documentation. It helps in reducing chaos and minimizes rework. Co-location also imbibes trust and mutual respect among the teammates that forms the basis to rationalized, rapid, and matured product development. It benefits in terms of lowering the capital & operational expenditure with simpler team management.

One of the projects that I got an opportunity to work way back in 2005 was to adopt agile in a pilot mode for a leading bank in the USA. Those days, when the organization and teams embarked on the agile journey, first and the foremost thing was to constitute a co-located team, as directed by the principles of agile. Still, this paradigm changed rapidly in the last few years, with the teams moving from co-location to virtual co-location. The teams are becoming more global in a real sense than just being local.

Software companies continue to embrace outsourcing and offshoring models, as they are on a roll for M&A (Mergers & Acquisitions), vendor consolidation, and expansion. But, the question remains to extract productivity and cost efficiency from their scattered teams. The groups are spread across the globe, and there is no mix/blend among themselves as they work in silos. It is tricky and tough for the engineering manager/leader to work out agile methodology with such strewn scrum teams.

They are unable to effectively achieve the aim to rapidly build software with superior quality, chiefly when the colleagues in the team are situated at different latitudes & longitudes. The leaders continue to face the barriers and roadblocks to building a genuinely global, well-blended project team in which the team members are stationed in different geographical locations.

Capitalize local with global team and talent

The global team consists of team members from two or more geographical locations. They could be distributed in terms of office branches located in different areas, towns, cities, countries, timezones, or continents. As an engineering manager, you should strive to create and lead such teams. There will be initial hiccups during the initial stages, during the team formation and normalization phase, but can transform into a breakthrough and a high-performance team gradually.

There are many reasons for the leadership to go for distributed teams in today's era. Some of the prominent ones are scarcity of talent at the same location with lack of skillsets, tax benefits on the software development cost in specific geographies, high operational costs in metropolitan cities, political instability, data privacy restrictions across boundaries, and many more. The companies are mitigating their risks by not restricting themselves to one single location for their research and engineering. Instead, they are spreading their presence and footprint across the globe.

The global agile teams bring in more opportunities compared to the challenges that it has. The organization increases its global mark by expanding its footprint in different geographies. It gets the finest of the talent in different places, which is otherwise difficult to find in the same location. This setup brings in different perspectives and thinking process to solve the same problem. It facilitates teams to deliberate from all possible angles healthily, benefiting the product.

Localization matters a lot in the product creation process, the team members from different demographics will have a better knowledge of their respective local market and customer needs in which you plan to sell it or expand your existence. Such familiarity and knowledge becomes very handy and can be utilized to build bespoke functionality for a particular geography and market in the product and tap the opportunities.

Follow the sun

The other significant benefit obtained is round the clock coverage in terms of development and customer assistance. Having the development team to work in 'follow-the-sun' mode, allows product building rhythm to maintain when one group finishes their day, and the other one comes in. The progress speeds up as the work is handed off from one team to another, resulting in a 24-hour development cycle. The clock duration to build a component reduces by 67%, approximately 1/3rd of the time that it would take if the entire team is situated at the same location or in the same time zone.

Leveraging 24 hours round the clock, with the follow-the-sun model, plays a pivotal role where your development shop never stops and keeps generating the software code. This mode was initially embraced by companies to provide customer service and support around the globe. But, now it has been adopted by the product development firms as well to build and ship the software to the market at a faster rate. It has become one of the crucial criteria for mergers and acquisitions, so that they can complement and enhance their product catalog & offerings with the support services.

113

Tax benefit

Software development in some parts of the world makes the company eligible for a decent tax relief on the software development cost, as the company is generating employment in that zone. Expenditures for the development of the software are often capitalized for book purposes and amortized over the useful life of the software. It brings down the overall investment and the cost of the software product to a reasonable extent, improving profitability.

Being genuinely global brings in more avenues for the companies to fast-track their growth. The engineering teams become a catalyst for the extension as they can ideate, innovate, validate, and fail/succeed in quickly changing ecosystem with high adaptiveness and pace.

Build global teams with the right attitude

Change of mindset, building confidence among the team members, and effective collaboration are some of the critical challenges faced in building a global high-performance team. The hallmark of a good leader lies in his or her ability to unlearn old traditional habits of doing things and embrace the new methods. It is the ability to be flexible as per the need of the hour and deliver. They need to come out of their mind blockage in terms of building the composition of the team. Gone are the days when the entire team and all the supporting functions used to be co-located. It is now more distributed and more diverse.

Secondly, the engineering executives also need to accept failures and welcome it with an open mind. They need to build high tolerance for failures because fiascos are the stepping stone for triumph. They need to encourage the team to fail fast with less risk. Their minds should be stimulated and challenged again and again to experiment more without the fear of failure. The culture of continual learning and disseminating information should be fostered within the team so that they become more adept in applying the lessons in their endeavor of product development.

It also helps team members to build their listening and articulation skills, when it comes to exchanging their ideas, agreements, or disagreements. The intention of the engineering leader should be to create an open atmosphere for the minds to cultivate ideas, innovate, and experiment so that they can acclimatize to the complex business environment and build solutions with more considerable momentum.

Nothing can work unless there is a trust and camaraderie established between the teammates. It becomes tougher, especially when they are not physically co-located and cannot interact face to face. There will be a sense of doubt and distrust due to distance, diverse nationality, and background. It also becomes difficult for the leader/manager himself to delegate tasks, have alignment, and monitor progress. The team members will be unsure of the colleague's work progress if they are sharing their work on the same task. Communication becomes an obstruction due to differences in timezone and a thin overlap of the office timings. There will be questions in terms of the commitment of every team member if they are remotely located. The cultural and language differences also act as barriers to building trust and credibility.

Traditional ways of brainstorming and knowledge transition sessions are not practical with the distributed teams as sync-ups and partnerships between them will not be immediate, as it would have been in the case of co-location. There are many other issues with the geo-spread teams, and it needs to be worked out and solved one by one. Engineering leaders should take a systematic, stepwise approach to build a highly proficient global project team with patience. The challenges that are highlighted above should be addressed with thorough planning and using existing tools within the organization.

The teammates should take pride in being part of the global team and should feel as an integral part of it. They should challenge themselves and be self-driven to take up and solve complex engineering problems along with their colleagues in the team. The goal should be to instill the feeling of 'One Team' and not of 'An Individual Contributor.'

How should you start on it?

Co-locate at the beginning

First and foremost is to enable collaboration and open communication between the team members so that the trust and companionship start to build up.

Co-locate the team members initially, especially during the forming phase. Bruce Tuckman, in 1965, proposed the model of forming-storming-norming-performing for the team formation. These phases are inevitable for a team to take up challenges, cope with problems, work on solutions, deliver results and grow together. In the co-location model, the group traverses through all these phases and mature over a period. However, it is not the case for a globally distributed team. Thus, the initial co-location of team members is a must.

That is the time when the group meets and learns about challenges and opportunities together. They also agree to common goals set for the team and take up tasks accordingly. The team members, being new, tend to behave and work more independently, rather than collaborating with other colleagues. The information on the tasks assigned to them is also incomplete, for which they may assume some things on their own. Orientation and alignment are missing at this formation phase. The co-location, at this point, helps them to connect in person. The manager should facilitate more brainstorming, requirement understanding, and knowledge sharing sessions so that the teammates are comfortable and open up in sharing their views and thoughts freely.

The nature of the tasks, complexity, and the methodology to be taken for those tasks should be discussed in one room with everyone so that the teammates start aligning with the point of view, body language and non-verbal cues of their colleagues.

Storming is the next and a vital phase where they start working together as a group and sorts out the problems within themselves. There might be some initial conflicts with a few of them as they take some additional role and responsibility, but the team learns on their own to manage and sort that out. Thus, the initial forming and some time of the storming phase is very crucial for the teammates to start gelling among themselves. It is when they start trusting each other and build confidence in each other's work. They start considering themselves as part of the team, guiding and hand-holding each other in their tasks if anyone is stuck anywhere or is unable to complete it before the end of the sprint

The team members can then relocate to their respective locations, as the first ice of apprehension & doubt has broken, and now, they are much more comfortable interacting and collaborating from remote. You should make it a point for the team to meet once every quarter or every six months at any office location. The group, over the course, is transformed. It takes approximately 3 – 4 sprints for teams to complete the forming and storming phase.

In the normalization phase, they play on their strengths to turn around quick optimal solutions to aid product formation. You will witness that the disagreements and personality clashes are resolved on their own. Their spirit of co-operation develops, and they share a common goal to succeed, win together. They are now self-driven, knowledgeable, strive collectively to solve a problem, and thrive jointly to achieve extraordinary results. They hold commitment, ownership, and accountability, to devote persistent efforts and build an awesome product.

Command the iteration framework with TDD (Test-Driven Development)

TDD is a software development methodology which converges three activities in a recurring manner. i.e., Testing, Development, and Design (Refactoring of Code). The focus is on unit testing the code in parallel to writing it. Based on the requirements, the test cases are written first. The minimal lines of code are written to satisfy the requirement that should pass that test case. Now the same code is refactored to meet the standards and tested again. This cycle continues, and features are developed in small iterations. There are various tools available for TDD that also comes with the ability to continuously integrate the code as and when it is built & tested.

Constructing in TDD mode is slower for the team initially when they begin; however, through practice, they become seasoned to reap the benefits of it. Since testing is at the forefront of this methodology, the quality of code increases considerably with fewer bugs. It becomes practically difficult to achieve 100% test coverage at the end of development with thousand lines of code. It is always endorsed to start testing the lines of code in parallel to writing it. The introduction of bugs reduces substantially as the code and functionality is checked in each iteration. It is a lot easier for the developer to automate the unit tests in parallel and refrain from manual validations again and again.

TDD helps engineering teams to reduce wastage of efforts and time on rework, debugging the code and bug fixes, implying faster and rapid development. TDD proves extremely useful when small changes and enhancements are done in a product suite, without putting the overall design and integration at risk. TDD way of development is advantageous, as considerable coverage of the requirements through test cases will expose the failure and blocking zones in the software to solve at the nascent stage itself. The team will be hesitant in the start to take up TDD and also apprehensive about its outcome. Still, you, as an engineering manager, should encourage your team to embrace this development paradigm by emphasizing its gains in the longer run.

Craft a branching policy

A source-control branching strategy should be in place before the team embarks on the coding and development path. A right branch-merge strategy is crucial for the accomplishment of distributed and rapid software development. It enables the developers to work independently on their respective modules without having to worry about the code merging and breaking nightmare. It does not disrupt their work, time, and sets them up for more effective code collaboration.

The branching mechanism becomes more beneficial when the developers are dispersed geographically. The code merging should be seamless to prevent overriding of each other's code changes, and breaking of existing functionality. Branching policy varies from organization to organization and from product to product. It primarily depends on the production release sequence, feature development teams, sprint cycle, and production support in terms of defect fixes.

Picking the right-branching policy at the beginning makes a huge difference to the product quality, availability, and developer's productivity. Below are a few powerful branching ploys used by product teams, according to the fitment.

- *Trunk-based development is when the developers refrain from causing child branches and work directly on the master (trunk) branch. This approach is practical for smaller engineering teams, especially when the feature development and testing cycles are shorter.*

- *Release-based branching is when the developers will work on the branch created for each planned and past release. It makes sense for the teams whose products have a long-running development cycle. It is also appropriate for the product teams who maintain and supports multiple release versions of the software in the production ecosystem to support their customers.*

- *Feature-based branching is when there are child branches forked out from the master branch to develop each feature independently. These feature branches are merged back to master once the testing team provides the sign-off on the functionality.*

Integrate continuously

Once the branching method is prepared, there are ground rules to be socialized and followed by the team. It sets the foundation for continuous integration. It enables developers to integrate their incremental code changes, 'n' number of times in a day, into a shared repository. But these integrations cannot be random. The developer should ensure that the new functionality is not broken and will not bring down any working/existing features. It is attained through automated build tests that run as soon as the code is checked-in the branch. It will alert and fail the build integration at that point, if there are any errors or bugs in the delta code piece, thus avoiding defect leakages in the main branch of the product.

This continuous integration of the code, on a real-time basis, is a must to avoid manual consolidation and amalgamation from different developers into the same branch, which is otherwise more error-prone to override other running functionality. The engineering team should be trained to construct continuous integration and deployment pipeline. It transforms the pace of software development by assembling it more rapidly and cohesively. The products hosted on Cloud, Web, reap enormous benefits from this model, as they can act on the feedback from the customers quickly, and make suitable changes in their software to enhance customer experience and growth.

Do DevOps to streamline and be predictable

DevOps is an integral part of today's product development paradigm. DevOps is a methodology that combines development and operations to shorten the development life cycle enabling continuous delivery with higher software quality. It can be unified with any type of software development, but it delivers exponential success for software products that are cloud-native, mobile-based, or in web-hosted infrastructure. A DevOps pipeline typically consists of multiple steps that run in an automated, condition-based manner. These steps involve building binaries, semantic analysis, sanity testing, other quality checks & criteria before it is deployed to the intended environment.

The 2017 State of DevOps Report, found that high performing organizations practicing DevOps spend 21% less time on unplanned work and unnecessary rework, and 44% more time on new work than their peers, eventually lowering the development cost, boosting higher productivity, and reducing alignment interactions. In addition to faster delivery and operational support, DevOps brings in the standardization of processes, enforcement of best practices, collaborative working, satisfied, and more engaged teams. It also increases team flexibility and cross-skilling opportunities within the group. In short, it helps businesses to save money and time with better predictability and discipline.

DevOps provides agility to the business to transform and respond to market changes, which are more cumbersome and voluminous in transactions, and data flows mainly in eCommerce, banking, and healthcare sectors. It brings in monitoring capabilities of the systems running in production so that any degradation or malfunction can proactively be alerted and attended. As an engineering leader, you should implement DevOps using the tools, if it is not readily done in your organization. You should pilot it in your product development and promote its benefits and value it brings to the enterprise, teams, and stakeholders.

Automated testing is golden

Automated testing means using an automation tool or a robot to execute your test case suite. The computerized software can generate test data for the testing, compare expected and actual results, and produce detailed reports. Software product development requires the same test suite to be executed again and again.

These validation suites are primarily classified into three categories – Regression, Smoke, and Sanity. An automated test suite has multiple test scenarios and consequent test cases.

- *The smoke test suite consists of test scenarios and cases covering the significant functional flows and use cases.*

- *The sanity test suite will mostly have the happy paths and a few required test cases to uncover any blocker issue.*

- *The regression test suite has the situations that covers the entire product functionality and critical paths.*

Usually, these three test suites are re-played again and again before any minor/major release of the product or the hotfix/bug patch rollout. It will be time-consuming if done manually, and therefore automation of these test suites comes convenient, playing a significant role in reducing the testing and overall deployment time.

Once the test suite is automated, there is no human intervention required. These suites can also be plugged in the build pipeline itself and set it to run every time a new build is triggered. Agile teams should focus on getting these tests automated and keep the suite updated with the relevant test case and scenario, automating them within the same or in the subsequent sprint.

Ensure the access, infrastructure and build environments are in place

You should make sure that the required access to all environments, artifact storage, infrastructure, and application lifecycle management tools are available to all team members across locations. There should be no dependency on anybody, and they should be well-equipped to perform all the engineering tasks without any impediments. The team members must comply with the processes and agile ceremonies with no exception. It brings uniformity, standardization, and eliminates a sense of bias.

The manager should preferably have a checklist composing a list of all environments, accesses, logins, databases, virtual machines, distribution lists, etc. in place. It becomes instrumental during the onboarding and offboarding of any colleague from the team. It also reduces the unnecessary back & forth between the teammates and other supporting functions.

Sync up for today and tomorrow

Typically in a daily stand-up, the teams sync up on the tasks or work to target for that particular day, but in the scattered squad, you must have the stand-up ceremony at an overlap time that is convenient for all. You must also plan the recurrence in such a way that half of the time, it is suitable for one geo team and the remaining half for the other geo team. It should not exceed more than 15 – 20 mins. You should prefer to have the scrum master from the group itself if the dedicated scrum master is at a completely different location

125

altogether. It minimizes the communication overhead, hand-offs, and wait times. You should also discuss the tasks that are planned for the next day as well, so that any dependency or ask can be tackled in advance. It will remove obstacles that might crop up the next day for the colleague.

Allocate smartly

Smart work allotment is the key. You can assign a complicated feature to co-located teammates, as it will require continuous consultation and partnership. The features that are long-running in the development phase also fits well with the co-located team members. Smaller functions or stories should be delegated to the team members at different locations. These build tasks are relatively smaller and simpler to achieve. It also does not have much dependence on other colleagues and can be done in isolation. They might want to collaborate with others during the integration of these small components at a later stage. The work allocation in terms of new development and bug fixes should also be in rotation mode, to have all teammates have experience in dealing with it.

Radiate information and dashboard on big screens

Information radiators and visual dashboards are electronic displays that the team must place in a highly visible location. The teammates and passers-by must be able to see the latest information related to the project or build at a glance. It may showcase the build health, failed test cases, sprint velocity, burndowns, task boards, storyboards, defect convergence in terms of open vs. closed, continuous integration status, and so on.

These dashboards can be created in the ALM tools itself using their out-of-box widgets. The link of these consoles should be shared with the team members at their respective locations to have a quick and real-time view of all vital parameters. They should also have immediate access to the tasks, defects, and stories assigned to them. These dashboards are pretty effortless and straightforward to create with a one-time effort. The widgets and graphs in the dashboard auto-populate with the real-time feed, at a set interval. These information radiators and dashboards help to keep the team focused and attentive on the critical paths and areas of immediate urgency. It also provides relevant clarity and transparency, not only to the engineering teams but also to the senior executives.

Have the right brainstorming kit handy

White-boarding and sticky notes with colorful marker pens still rocks in a team's bay. It is a quick canvas to discuss, draw and brainstorm anything on design, approach, plan, or schedule. It helps in having quick discussions where more team members are required. It becomes handy when the team is in a war room to fix a burning problem in the production environment. Quick diagrams and flowcharts with the right color scheme can make a vast difference in nailing down the measures and solutions. Some of the ALM tools also have the feature of an electronic whiteboard, which can be used by team members from different locations. Many thoughts, conflicts on a particular design or implementation approach can be sorted out using the whiteboard and sticky notes. The best part of these tools is that the team members, who are shy and are not so vocal about their point of view, contribute openly through these channels, which is much easier and more comfortable for them. In this way, we do not lose on their ideas and suggestions.

These are my favorite tools when it comes to brainstorming and designing with my team. I keep them handy in my bay and also carry a few colored marker pens and sticky notes in my bag. I have already shared about the importance of the mind mapping technique in my earlier chapter. Nothing works out well as the whiteboard and colored marker pens during such open-ended sessions.

Build connects within the distributed team

Collaboration is a must, and tools to make it useful is a necessity for the success of engineering teams. Teammates need to work in tandem with each other to build the right product and test in tandem. Efficacious collaboration in agile leads to better results with fewer misunderstandings and revisions. It results in faster product development and delivery.

Getting architects, designers, and engineers on the same page is not easy, especially when they are dispersed. That is the reason why the right tools become an absolute need to enable meaningful collaboration and communication between team members across the geographies. These collaboration tools became extremely vital during the Coronavirus outbreak in 2020 when the teams were working remotely from home. Offices across the world were shut due to lockdown to maintain social distancing and break the virus chain spread. Tools like Zoom and Microsoft Teams witnessed a significant surge in their usage. These were the only mediums to connect with colleagues and team members.

There are ALM (Application Lifecycle Management) tools to manage the lifecycle of a product from concept to the sunset phase. The primary aim of these tools is to capture and trace the entire journey of the product - requirements, design, proof of concepts minimum viable product iterations, releases, defects, backlog, etc. These are hosted centrally with a shared repository with all the product and project-related artifacts. Atlassian products like Confluence and JIRA are principally used by the scrum teams to manage their development phases and histories. Most of these tools are on the cloud, making it easier for groups across locations to use it. They are integrated effortlessly with different IDEs and tools through plugins, code repositories like GitHub, integration pipeline like Jenkins, code analysis tools like SonarQube, Blackduck, testing tools, and content & artifact storage like Confluence or SharePoint. The team should be trained on these ALM tools so that they take up and leverage it for adding tempo and speed in their work.

Set ground rules for communication

Communication in geographically distributed teams is less frequent without much of face to face conversations. There should be some ground rules to follow. The collaboration model with the tool should be decided and ensured that all the team members are equipped with it. Video of all team members should be on so that they can have superior interaction looking at the non-verbal cues and expressions.

The meetings should be time-bound facilitated by someone. It should have a clear agenda topics and the objective to each point. The organizer or facilitator should ensure that the team members listen attentively and do not cut over each other to dominate the conversation. The manager should also make a point to plan a few time-offs like virtual coffee breaks or off-work slots, where the team can talk, share, and collaborate on something other than their jobs. It supports sharing their interests and cross-pollination of information.

Team members should be open and comfortable to share what is going well for them and what is not, what are the challenges that they face so that they can get suggestions from other colleagues. Team building exercises should be performed often to celebrate and have fun. These aspects build team dynamics to a different level. The ultimate intent is to have the team feel integrated, connected, and part of one family, though they are remotely stationed at various locations.

Chapter 7

Cultivate an 'all-rounder' team

"Alone, we can do so little; together, we can do so much." These were the words by renowned American author, activist, and lecturer, Helen Keller. It meant that an individual could achieve only so much alone. But if you are a group of self-motivated individuals with the thirst to grow together, then the sky is the limit. The hallmark of an all-rounder team is a group of individuals sharing one vision & goal, striving to achieve it in collaboration, confronting obstacles to accomplish breakthrough results.

Building such teams is a lifetime opportunity for any leader. A great team cannot be created by merely hiring outstanding candidates. Filling the roles with people is not going to make a high-performance team. Most of the time, the engineering manager does not have the luxury to select members for your group. Usually, you are given a team and are expected to deliver the expectation with the same team. There is much more that it takes to nurture stronger teams in any organization, and the leadership must play the catalyst role to make it happen.

The leadership should take strides with patience and perseverance to build an all-rounder team.

Align the team to a single vision and goal

First and foremost is to have a clear vision and goal outlined. More often, the team members are designated on multiple projects and unplanned work simultaneously. The timelines of these projects and tasks are varying with different expectations and stakeholders. They all have urgency too. It creates confusion and chaos.

The colleagues burn out working on multiple projects and ad-hoc tasks with no apparent result and achievement. The ability to focus on a single project from planning to completion is the key to high performance. But in reality, the team is loaded with several unplanned work that the focus is lost, and the dedicated work goes for a toss. This is not a sustainable way to execute the project and definitely, not in favor of the team performance as well. You need to ensure that the team is concentrated and working only on the planned job.

There should be a single point of contact from the team; undoubtedly, the development manager for all the work or asks that routes from different stakeholders, including product owners. The development manager is the one who knows the team's workload, capacity, and the overall plan that they are in pursuit of. He/she must prioritize and set the right expectations with the stakeholders.

Saying NO is of utmost prominence. You cannot agree to take up everything that comes on your plate. That's the reason the engineering/development manager needs to know the most delicate details of the requirement and its probable implementations. The entire team should never be exposed to the stakeholders, except for the development manager, who should be the only face and point of contact for the world outside the project. It supports the team to stay engaged and on track.

Balance and distribute the opportunities

Distribute opportunities equally among the team members - Treat all the teams and team members alike. Ensure that you do not treat the vendor's team members separately. The amount and the complexity of the workload must be distributed evenly. The problem statement should be discussed with everyone, and ideas/solutions should be sought from them. The engineering manager must ensure that the team members are actively participating in all discussions and devising sittings. Their inputs must be listened to with an open mind.

The ownership and accountability of the components that are being developed by vendor teammates should be with them so that they feel an integral part of the team. Every resource in the team should be optimally utilized with the workload and functionality to develop. Work assignments should have a balanced distribution among the group. Rotate the roles and responsibilities like scrum master, RCA champion, or defect triaging facilitator, etc., so that everyone gets a chance to experience it. In this way, they learn to manage their time in working on both coding and other tasks simultaneously.

Trainings and seminars should be organized on technical, domain, and processes for the team to keep them in constant touch with the academia and industry-embraced best practices. They will be up to speed on the latest and greatest happenings in their space. Cross-functional and cross-component opportunities should be provided to the teammates so that they can learn and share varied technologies while applying and become full-stack engineers.

The maintenance and distribution of opportunities in equilibrium brings in optimism, confidence, and control in the team.

Challenge your team to unleash their potential

Challenge your team to unleash their potential. "Before you are a leader, success is all about growing yourself. When you become a leader, success is all about growing others" these are the words of wisdom from former CEO of General Electric, Jack Welch. As an engineering leader, you should continuously strive to get the best out of your team. Every colleague possesses different skill sets, logical reasoning, problem-solving tactics, and analytical ability. They will be outstanding in some areas but average in others. Managers should challenge their teammates endlessly so that they do not get complacent at any time and should not be satisfied merely with the work allocated to them.

The squad should be on a continuous thinking spree for solving the engineering problem or the task. The leader should provide the necessary support to the team members and set them up for success. While challenging your team, you should also express your belief in their potential and set the bar of expectation high enough to keep them out of their comfort zone. You need to prepare them to take risks but fail safely. The typical tendency of humans is to be easily satisfied with what they are doing. But this contentment should never be in the DNA of a high-performance team.

They should incessantly drive to improve and add value. The teammates who will be taking up the challenge head-on might fail at times. It is not possible that they will succeed always, and that is when they will need your support. You need to be behind them and get them back up by motivating and tutoring them to learn from that failure. They need to learn to embrace collapses in the stride to innovate and grow. As a leader, you should stand by your team for every downside that they face in their product creation journey. They should be reassured repetitively about your support.

Intellect is one facet, but the relentless effort with the rigor to grow continuously is the key. Intelligent people are not necessarily adept at handling stressful situations. They are vulnerable, scared of breakdowns, and sometimes even in the state of denial to accept any deficiencies and areas of improvement. Persistent rigor, discipline, and hard work is more important than the talent, hence you, as a leader, should always appreciate the effort and the scheme with which they work. It takes arduous efforts to master anything and when recognized, motivates, & energies other co-players as well.

Encourage your team to participate in coding competitions and hackathons. Push them to write blogs, POVs (Point of Views), take seminars on the new learnings and experience that they gain in terms of technology, domain, or process. Urge them to take up certifications or online courses that are relevant to their work, and interest. Coming out of a comfort zone and devoting extra effort & time in such activities is very tough. You should continuously persuade and guide them to promote their work and thoughts in larger forums and outside company boundaries. In this way, they will contribute to the broader tech community. It will widen their knowledge horizon and will make them more confident in their work and achievements.

Leverage individual's forte

A strong team needs individuals with strong skills, intellect, and relentless rigor to conquer. But that's not all; multiple other factors matter considerably and bring difference in the team. Some individuals are detail-oriented, and others are a pro at creating the end-to-end high-level picture. Few can articulate their views/suggestions cogently, and few are incredibly creative in making diagrams and flowcharts to depict their ideas. Certain colleagues can think strategically, and others are skilled in tactical planning and implementation. A few can build good relationships, while others are proficient in written communication.

The essence of a great team is to possess all these diversified traits to complement each other. There might be some weaknesses and shortcomings that an individual might have, but these limitations disappear when they are ONE TEAM. It also offers the team a platform to learn from each other, exchange their views, deliberate, and excel together.

Shield your team from the nuisance and noise

Removing distraction is the first element in building alignment within a fully operational and functional team, which also helps them to grow inside out. Time and again, the team will be exposed to the different challenges in their product development journey. It is a VUCA world in software development where there is volatility, uncertainty, complexity, and ambiguity. It is difficult for the business to have a rock-solid path without any tests. Business and leadership has to deal with multiple variables that impact the team's work and pace. The key is to have a bright outlook on all these changing variables and have transparency with the team.

The development manager and leadership should provide an amicable atmosphere to their teams for innovation to perform their job with the highest standard. Stakeholders who are themselves short of clarity and knowledge tend to add noise and unnecessary confusion to the team. They may also try to influence the team and the stakeholders. They will infiltrate in the operational path of the engineering team with their unwanted proposals. The challenge is to keep such a nuisance at large. You can affiliate with these stakeholders around the vision and the goal.

Inform such individuals about the focussed business values that the team is acting on, and that may help them to get aligned. But if not, then the team should be shielded from all such disturbances and distractions. If, at a certain point, it is not under your circle of influence, you need to highlight this to the leadership through a suitable channel and governance matrix to curb this at the early stage itself. There may be personalities (especially peacocks and panthers) who would openly blame or finger point the team or colleague, where you need to step in and guard them with appropriate factual data and details.

As an engineering manager, you should have the ownership on any lapses or if a ball dropped somewhere. But you should safeguard your team in all the circumstances. You should certainly have a quick conversation with your team to have corrective and preventive measures in place to avoid such errors again.

Nurture trust and team character

Trust is supreme in a great team. Lack of faith slows down everything. An open environment is where you can cultivate great minds and talent. The unit cannot succeed if there is no mutual respect and admiration for their colleague's work and effort. It will get imbibed gradually over time. The team goes through different stages of formation to reach the final stage of high performance, as put forward by a renowned psychologist Bruce Tuckman. I have talked about it in my previous chapter.

The first stage is forming where most team members are positive and polite; some are anxious as they lack clarity on the work, and rest are merely excited about the work. At this point, the development manager must play a dominant role in providing them the clarity and information about their roles and responsibility. Keep in mind, the team is just formed and is in the blossoming stage. Therefore, you should not expect the team to self-organize at this phase. You will have to show them the goal and the roadmap to reach there. This stage takes some time as the teammates start working with their colleagues and understanding them as well.

Next stage is storming, where the teammates start to have conflict due to their natural working styles. It is the stage where the teams might fail. People will have different styles of working, and that is perfectly alright; however, the problem arises when these working variations cause issues and impact on the product eventually. It adds negativity, frustration, and resentment. Some of the teammates might get overwhelmed with the workload while others are uncomfortable with the working style of others. Few may resist picking up tasks on their own, and few others may lose focus on the goal in the midway. Few of the teammates, at times, may behave rude and unrealistic, cutting down others and insensitive to other's viewpoints. At times, they may also not hesitate to question your authority and the basis of the decisions that you have been taking.

The critical lesson for the manager is to have continuous dialogue and conversations with them in the storming phase. You need to understand the root cause of the problem from the teammate's perspective and tackle to resolve it completely.

Norming is the next stage after storming, where the team progressively moves to a steady-state. It is where the teammates resolve their differences, respect, and admire a colleague's effort & strengths. They also begin to accept you as a leader. In this stage, they know each other better, mingle and hang out together with more openness to ask help from each other. They also develop a stronger bond and commitment towards the team objectives and provide constructive recommendations. You should offer them space and time to resolve conflicts and differences among themselves and pitch in, if required.

The last stage is performing, where there is negligible friction, and the team collaborates and performs collectively. The team will do process and roadmap conformance with precision and desire. It is the stage where, as a manager, you can start giving them ownership and a free hand to make decisions on their own. It will not only boost their rate but will also bring in accountability at work. It is where the team is now on the path of delivering the highest quality product and can rightfully claim to be an 'all-rounder' team. Trust and confidence are rooted in the team's DNA at this juncture.

Team dynamics shape the character of the entire squad to achieve an astonishing feat or make them mediocre. It is the time. If the blend is right, they will accomplish their mark with synergy by crossing all the obstacles in their path. Open and honest dialogue between the colleagues lifts the dynamics and texture of the team.

As a leader, you should consistently attempt to build a positive environment and relationships amongst the team and yourself. You should always hunt for avenues to develop and showcase the team's potential and capabilities. The leader or the manager should always be consistent in his actions, speech, and stay true to his pledges made to the team.

Have direct connect

Having direct connect with your team is of massive importance to build trust and faith. You should have frequent one-on-one dialogue with each teammate and appreciate their efforts. You should reward them for their efforts and achievements promptly and create visibility for them in front of senior executives and leadership. You should also connect with them often and more, during lunches, coffee breaks, watercooler, and off-working time.

You should not bound yourself to chat only about the product or the deliverables but utilize the time to have performance-specific discussions, career grooming, coach them to use their expertise, and fields where they can improve and scale. Everyone wants to have evident expectations and direction in their goals, and these are the moments when you can provide them a roadmap, course correction to make them more constructive in their future endeavor. You should not wait for the official yearly appraisal meetings to share your inputs or provide guidance. The coaching should be a continuous process on the ground. These rendezvous must happen at regular intervals for the team to have rhythm & rigor to realize the vision of the product and the company.

Reward and recognize efforts promptly

Who does not like to be rewarded or acknowledged for their achievements? Everyone! Right? Rewards and recognition are something that are missed out or are not paid heed by the leadership. Many companies either do not see any value in recognizing their employees. Management is busy with the bigger picture of achieving company goals and complete projects. The leaders tend to forget in their daily work chores, or they do not feel the need for it. But one fundamental aspect overlooked is that the people are the greatest asset in a company, primarily in software services and product development units.

I firmly believe that it is a very critical facet in any working environment, and their needs to be a plan around it as well. It hardly takes any time to write a few words of appreciation or speak informally for a colleague/team who has gone beyond their commitment to achieve a remarkable feat and deliver value. Recognition plays an essential part in boosting an individual's and team's productivity, resulting in the company's growth.

Teams must always be motivated, energized, and confident in taking risks, generate innovative ideas & solutions, to achieve results that matter. A high-performing team goes beyond all the tests, and you, as an engineering leader, you must back them with everything that they need. Never let your team be down or feel low. There will be times when they will fail or will have no direction; that is the time when, as a leader, you need to consult, inspire them, and ensure your presence around them. Remember, a true leader is the one who is the face during failures but makes his team stand on the podium when there are accomplishments.

You should facilitate discussions to come up with alternative options to solve an issue or improve the product development voyage. The engineering manager needs to be more of a mentor than a manager to the team. Help them proactively wherever they are stuck, and remove the hindrances in their path. It will keep them high on their commitment and focus. You should recognize and reward their effort through an informal/formal announcement or an award. You can also choose to write an email thanking them for their contribution and share it with senior executives to provide prominence.

You should utilize your one-on-one dialogue with your teammates to get the pulse on their feeling about the work, colleagues, and management. Talk about their aspirations and their personal career goals. Keep these chats as open and as honest as possible. Hear their concerns out with adequate attention. You must coach them to grow not only in the current enterprise but also overall in their career and future stints. Small gestures, like taking them out for dinner or coffee, also makes a difference in building healthy connect.

It is a must for the team that they are backed up by their manager, and have assurance that he/she is always there to support them in any consequences. Never lose an opportunity to showcase the team's effort in your chats or meetings with the management. It opens up more avenues for the team in the future.

Building the brand of the team internally in the corporation is also necessary. You should always keep challenging your team with some organization-level task or a need where they can pitch and provide solutions to it. You should involve them in contributing to initiatives that run across functions and teams. Speak about your team's achievements and milestones in different company forums and conferences. You should actively participate and set up booths in the exhibitions and tech expos organized.

The colleagues feel positive and highly determined to excel in their tasks and improve at every step, if their efforts are recognized. Your squad should be aware of how their hard work is bearing fruits for the company and is adding value to the product and business.

Finally, never miss an occasion to thank their families and friends for all the sacrifices they make and allow willingly to let them work and focus without adding any distractions. Your product and program cannot succeed without the unconditional backing and co-operation of their family.

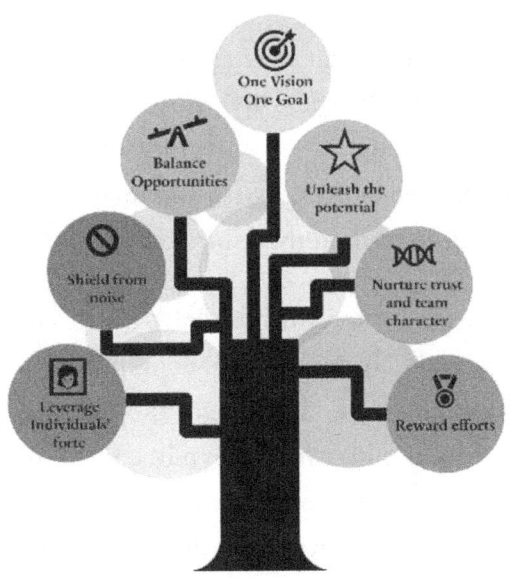

Work on listening competence

Listening is an indispensable part of our life, but we, humans, do not realize the importance of it. I firmly believe, listening is a skill that you cannot develop overnight; it takes years of practice, dedication, and focus on achieving it. You will always come across great speakers, but you will hardly find great listeners. A good leader is an excellent listener. They speak very less, crisp and to the point. They listen to all the viewpoints and ultimately choose one after evaluating all the possible options in their mind. Listening makes you a better human being and, indeed, an effective leader and decision-maker.

Today, everyone wants to be heard, but they hardly want to listen. Part of being an excellent communicator means knowing how to listen first. The communication cycle fails when there is only talking and no listening. Studies suggest that the person hears between 20,000 to 30,000 words, on an average daily. Listening could be in any form, e.g., listening to music, watching TV, while talking to someone, listening to sounds and noise from the surrounding, etc. Studies reveal that 70 to 80% of the waking hours are consumed in some form of communication, of which 45% is listening. Yet, we are poor listeners.

If we are spending almost half of our time listening, then why are we poor listeners?

There are multiple reasons for it. One of the core reasons being we are never taught about listening in our school. While much of the focus is spent on reading, writing, and speaking, there were no classes on the subject of listening in school, right from the primary section. I am sure that the curriculum designers and teachers must have thought about this, but there was no specific attention and attempt to teach how to be a better listener.

Perhaps there is a perception that intelligent students are good listeners, and others lack it. I remember one of the ways my teachers use to ensure that we listen, was by making us sit on the first/second-row benches in rotation. That way, everyone in the class sits in the front and pays attention to what teachers are teaching. This arrangement did not matter for me and some of my friends as we use to pretend still to listen without paying attention. It was presumed that reading would teach you listening also, but that's not true. Research has proved that reading and listening skills do not develop at the same rate when the attention is only on reading. The fact is, a small or, rather, no consideration is given to improve the listening skills in the school curriculum itself, gradually degrading and eventually faltering it completely.

I remember my first formal training on listening abilities was done when I stepped into the corporate world. At first, I was a bit anxious and inquisitive to know the aspects that will be covered in this listening course. Still, it turned out to be an eye-opener for me when our trainer highlighted the benefits of this undervalued ability that we all possess. The training was exciting, informative, and engaging. It consists of role-plays and scene-enactment that helped us to relate most of the stuff in our real-life. It also gave us a good insight into the motives and benefits of listening in our corporate world.

Listening is something that we use the most in our daily routine, but we do not use it effectively. Developing good listening ability is essential, especially when it comes to building professional and personal relationships. In this chapter, I will keep it confined only to professional life. We work closely with our colleagues, teammates from different social backgrounds, academia, language, culture, and geographies. They come with varied work experiences.

Hearing forms the base to connect with your colleagues and build trust and compassion. The more you listen, the better you understand, and you empathize with them. The flow of thoughts is deficient unless somebody hears you raptly. It helps you to identify a person's mind and intent. The outcome of conversations is more productive when both parties listen carefully.

Listening effectively also prevents mistakes and rework. In many occasions, we realize that it reduces the wastage of the team's time and work, if they listen actively to the suggestions and feedback in the requirement grooming and demo sessions. Often, in war rooms, when there is more urgency to solve a scorching customer problem, it is observed that communication is happening only in one direction, i.e., everyone is talking, but none are listening. An apt and a quick resolution suggested by someone in the room at that instance, might go unnoticed, delaying the fix to the issue.

There are several rationales for not being an active listener.

Distracted listening

Distracted listening is when we are not entirely focusing on what the person is speaking. It happens when we are multi-tasking during meetings or discussions, distracted on what is happening outside the room/office or something internal to you, which is bothering you, e.g., hunger. There are always internal and external distractions that surround us. You may miss an important point or a problem that the person is trying to highlight.

Biased motives

We enter a conversation with hidden motives, a bias thought, or a preconceived judgment in our mind. In this case, we are not actively listening to the person; instead, we are just waiting to invade abruptly and put across our point. In a technical design review with an architect, the presenter will try and defend his design and plan carved out by him. Instead, the presenter should get the design reviewed with an open mind to accept comments, and seek suggestions to improve it further. If there is prejudice for your work without the willingness to receive feedback from others, then that work can never get better. It is where the communication fails, and the outcome is of mediocre quality.

Emotional listening

Emotional listening is something that you will often witness. During our connect with the co-workers or seniors, there are, at times, when we fear something, or someone. The feeling of superior creeps in unknowingly while having a dialogue with your teammates. You will be worried to highlight the project delays to your engineering VP, and possibly you may not reveal the real root cause for the delay. You may dominate and probably loud when you are discussing the same delay with your team. The attitude and tone of the conversation change with the ability to listen, as per the situation and members. In both cases, the desired outcome is not attained, which is to come up with the mitigation plan to restraint further delays in the project.

Jumping to judgments

We tend to assume things and jump to conclusions. We lack patience to hear out the entire point of the speaker, leading to misaligned understanding and confusion. It often leads to emotion-driven altercations. Some people lack in conveying their opinions efficiently, resulting in misunderstanding and confusion. Therefore, you should certify your assumption with the speaker before concluding your assessment on it. Half baked knowledge is always dangerous. Consequently, you should abstain from rushing to inferences without having the detailed insight on it.

Now, we know about the significance of listening and the vulnerabilities that inhibit us from being active listeners. We should make a conscious effort to listen genuinely. Give your time and attention. It should be apparent to the speaker that you are genuinely interested in his words. Passive listening or pretending to hear is more dangerous than not listening at all. At least the speaker does not get the wrong impression that you agree with him when, in reality, you are not.

Listen attentively

Ideally, if you ponder, we should hear twice as much we speak as God has gifted us two ears and one mouth. Devote your time in listening and understanding the point the person is trying to make. Never jump to suppositions quickly. Corroborate your assumptions and check if your perception is aligned with the speaker. The diversions must be averted altogether. Try not to carry your laptop in meetings and keep your phones out of your sight in the silent mode.

Keep the spotlight on speaker

In reality, during any conversation, the emphasis is typically on us and not on the speaker, and somewhere we keep contemplating in our subconscious mind on when to agree or disagree, without hearing the point assiduously. Our mind is in a constant haste to put across our position. Instead, the focus and limelight should be on the speaker. Grasp from their frame of reference and thinking. Be attentive to their body language, facial gestures, and try to decode the hidden cues and implicit meaning/intent that the speaker is trying to make. Voice modulation of the presenter will also give you the intensity and insight on the message that he wants to convey.

Understand the implicit message

We get upset and offended when our manager conveys his/her discontent and frustration to us if there is a production collapse or the customer raises a critical issue. The real cause of this exasperation is the defect, that is impacting the customer's business and in turn, our company's reputation and business. It may not be called out by the manager explicitly. But, the high tone is a sign for the team to determine the gravity and urgency of the problem. Understanding underlying thoughts, emotions, needs, and being sensitive towards it, builds the confidence and faith in the team. After all, it takes years to build the trust, seconds to break and forever to repair it.

Paraphrase and validate

Paraphrasing and condensing your interpretation is a crucial step to become an active listener. It gets you alignment with the speaker. You should also request for more information wherever you feel. This way, it will build not only faith but also camaraderie and a healthy work environment.

Listening peacefully helps you to gather simplicity in your thoughts, preventing chaos and clutter. Experts recommend that we should listen to ourselves and introspect for 10 – 15 minutes daily. Many choose to meditate to enhance their concentration and reflect on feelings within themselves. Listening to yourself first will make you a better listener for others.

Always seek to understand first before being understood, as listening is the missing half of the communication.

Chapter 8

Quality is paramount

Product quality is supreme, and there are no second thoughts around it. It can make or break the product acceptance in the market. It could be a catalyst for a company's skyrocket growth or its crash. Quality is one division where every software team combats to meet it. It is also the department where it could be friction and chaos if the quality goals are not expounded. It is quality that defines the product persona. For example, you download a new app on your smartphone today, and you start using it until you realize that it has many bugs.

To begin with, the loading of the app takes time; the app gets frozen in between, the usability and navigation in the app is not easy and intuitive. It randomly gets crashed, wiping off the data that you have entered. What will you do next? You would immediately delete the app from your phone. Now even if the company fixes all the infested defects, the awful user experience will prevent you to re-install it. With social media and online platforms, this negative experience will take no time to spread across the user community, impacting the brand and reputation of the company.

Quality takes precedence over everything in software product development. It can never take a back seat or be compromised. The quality builds the brand name of the product, and the enterprise, creates stickiness between the product and its users. Multiple research has converged on inferior quality as the main reason for the downfall of the software products in the market. The primary origin for inferior quality is the absence of a robust testing strategy, adequate coverage, and stringent quality tests. Software testing experts are mindful of the reason, yet they find it daunting to fix it.

A few tests that the product development unit confronts today are

- *Inability to accelerate testing to cope up with the fast-paced product development and deployment*
- *Cultivate testing culture and empowering testers*
- *Absence of right testing strategy – Shift left and automation*
- *Lack of suitable quality assurance management, tools and methodologies*
- *Dearth of thorough impact and feasibility analysis*
- *Good testing coverage for a complex technology stack*

Engineering leaders in charge of developing software are under enormous pressure to boost development velocity and, at the same time, enrich quality. Today, the software development pace has increased multi-fold. Gone are the days when the code was pushed to production in three or six months. Today, binaries are being promoted to production at a weekly, daily, and or even at an hourly rate. Amazon, for example, unfolds new software for production every 11.7 seconds through its automated deployment service. Faster time to market is a prerequisite today for any software company to succeed and have a competitive advantage over its rivals. Study shows that the high-performing product development shops deploy software 30 times more frequently, with 200 times shorter lead times.

You can now correlate to how the quality of the software will be impacted with such quick release cycles and development rotations. The next thing that comes to our mind is that there will be more defects and bugs added in the product, if we speed up the deployment. But that is not always the case. It is a two-edged sword. You cannot afford to delay your releases until 100% quality checks are passed, and you also cannot hurry on deployments without performing all the quality checks. Thus, there should be a balanced and an apt plan laid out for it. Remember, quality should always be at the forefront of your product strategy and objective.

Creating a testing mindset and culture is the first thing to be done. Testing is not the final stage in the development cycle anymore as it used to be during the earlier waterfall days. Now, with agile, testing is continuously performed along with the development. Test cases are penned in parallel with the functional design. Validation and testing is an on-going step in agile software development pattern. A story cannot be marked completed and done unless it is put to the test, and all the bugs specific to that story are solved.

I have noticed that some engineering functions tweak the definition of done as per their convenience, but in my view, it should not change. A story should be marked 'Done' only post validation with all the blockers and critical defects addressed.

Testers must participate from the beginning

Testers must be an active contributor in the story grooming ceremony. They need to know the design, architecture, and the files in which the functionality will be programmed. They cannot be just testing it as a black box and provide the results. A good tester is one who not only examines the functionality end to end but also analyzes the potential root cause of the surfaced defects. Testing is a collective team effort. Each teammate should be in the sphere right from the beginning of the project and should participate keenly. Giving testers access to requirements and design early on will assist them in preparing test scenarios, cases, environments and testbeds. It will provide them enough time to think through all possible angles and account them in their test strategy to thwart risks and delays in the future.

Unit testing, make it a habit

Code manufacturers typically abstain from comprehensively unit-testing their code in haste to provide their element. The benchmark for unit test code coverage is a very crucial metric that a developer must adhere to at the time of coding itself. It varies from 85 – 95%, depending on the quality maturity and requirements of the product function. It must be enforced systemically that the unit-test code coverage conforms to the set threshold, before its submission in the trunk branch. Code manufacturers can achieve this only when the written test cases are relevant, automated, and easy to run. They should be incorporated with the IDE (Integrated Development Environment) itself that they use for programming.

Abstain from gold plating

155

Gold plating is a phenomenon that we all engineers do. Gold plating is adding a bonus feature or functionality which is not asked or expected by the customers. You, as an engineering leader, should ensure that there is no gold plating done at all. It comes with an additional effort and cost, both from the development and testing perspective. Also, once the feature is deployed in production, it needs to be always supported and maintained. It proves to be cost-ineffective to develop a feature that is not asked for and then attach a recurring cost to it for its maintenance. The team needs to understand that there should always be an ROI (Return on Investment) outlined before designing a functionality.

Comprehensive testing strategy is a must

In the ideal world, we all try to build a 100% perfect software without any bugs in it. But it is not practically feasible. The software industry cannot operate in a zero-defect mode, and will not sustain with that philosophy. There are various underlying levers in the form of business priorities, and competitive landscape, that leads you to have an optimal testing policy. The policy should make sure that the software meets & supports the needs of your customer with a satisfying user experience. It also propels the engineering team to accomplish the right quality within the expected timeframe. The emphasis must not be on writing a large number of test cases. Instead, attention should be on writing an optimum amount of test cases to have maximum coverage and efficacy. The strategy should be aligned with business stakeholders and the engineering team to set reasonable expectations.

156

COMPREHENSIVE TESTING STRATEGY

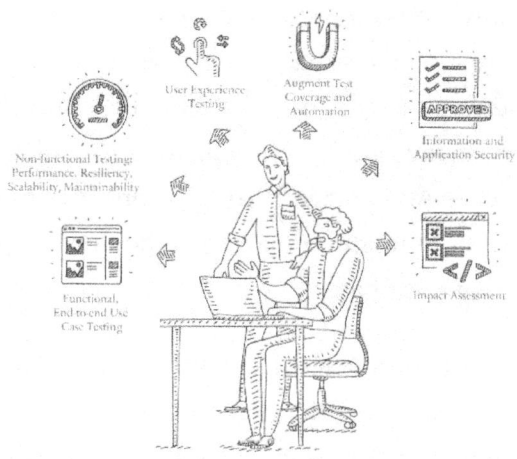

Documentation of testing strategy is a need at the start itself. Once the product roadmap and the program charter/plan are in place, the ensuing thing is to outline a testing strategy, an elaborate one. It then becomes a reference point for all the engineering teams to follow and adhere to it. The technical documentation, run books, NFR, production testing, and surveillance should be encompassed in the whole strategy. It should cover every aspect of product validation and certification. It must be assessed as well by the architects, technical leads, and product owners.

Test end-to-end customer use cases

We covered the bugs unearthed by the internal testing squad, but what about the ones raised by the customers. Production issues are expensive in terms of cost, time, and repute. The cause of such problems are many – missed test case of an end-to-end scenario or an oversight in component testing or a design flaw. Sometimes, we forget to include end-to-end use cases in the testing plan in the beginning, later to miss out in the end due to rush and timeline pressure. UAT (User Acceptance Testing) is one way to authenticate these cases; however, it might not cover all the flows in package with NFR testing during this phase.

Customer use cases and flow testing should be thought through and recorded separately, studying the user touchpoints and journey with the product. It must contain a step-wise sequence of every interaction with event triggers and maneuvers in the software. These flows must be illustrated in a visual storyboard for easy and quick grasp. It verifies user pattern and their usage of the software. Trigger-points prompting customers to use a specific product feature are of utmost importance. Knowing the device, platform, and the emotion with which they use the product is also vital in slicing out the right end-to-end test scenarios and user flows.

The ultimate target must be to automate the complete testing flows. However, you need to weigh in the effort for it against the future usage & coverage. Many times, the team elects to have a hybrid method in which most of the flows are programmed, and the remaining ones are left manual.

NFR testing equally important

NFR (Non-Functional Requirements) testing is something without which the testers should never provide the sign-off on the product or the feature. There are various types of NFRs to be considered. Still, as part of the testing strategy and end-to-end flow determination, the engineering and product team should identify NFRs relevant to the product/feature. Post that, a detailed scheme must be laid out to certify the NFRs. The associated setup should be in place, in terms of environment, data stubs, and tools. NFR testing requires various certification cycles, and therefore, the installation for NFR testing should be separate and not interfered with by functional testers.

In today's era, both in B2B (Business to Business) and B2C (Business to Consumers), the volume of users is massive. The data streams are no more in megabytes; they are, in fact, in Giga or terabytes. The testing team needs to be mindful of the expected volume of the users, amount of data, usage peak trend over a time frame, frequency of usage, traffic, etc. in production before they can come up with the plan. The users should not experience difficulties in terms of feature loading or the performance, driving them to look for an alternative elsewhere. Load, soak, chaos testing are some of the proven testing methodologies that cover the performance, scalability, availability, extensibility, etc. aspects of the software. These should be accounted in the plan, and executed using automation scripts post the component, and integration testing is done.

Augment test coverage

Maximizing test coverage through automation should be the underlying rule for all the testers in the team. The software application should be broken down into smaller components and flows to test them autonomously. By doing so, you will be able to check the field level validations. It will uncover more minor flaws and mismatches right in the development phase itself during the in-sprint testing, avoiding wastage of effort later. The preference should be to automate test cases for each component in the same sprint of its development. It benefits the testing team to have continued rigor to automate in parallel, and avoid piling it up.

Information security, equally vital

Information security and vulnerability testing should also be part of the testing stratagem. There are cutting-edge tools available in the market which conform to the industry best practices and standards in terms of data privacy and information security. The engineering team should leverage these tools to run scans on the product at every intermediate milestone, and resolve threats exposed by the tool, chiefly the intellectual property, operational, license, and information security risks.

Organize with a test management suite

The team should incorporate a test management suite for maintaining their test case repository and history of all previous tests. It must fit and cater to your product and business needs. There is not a single tool that will suit in all scenarios. The team should look at and evaluate the test management tool that should mainly serve two purposes. First - it should be easy to maintain the test scenarios, test cases, execution, and results. Secondly - to have the flexibility to alter the testing approach and implementation based on the future needs of the product to meet rapidly changing business requirements.

It should have easy reporting and dashboard capability to chart out reports and trends, for the team and stakeholders. A tester's time is valuable. The code examiners should not waste their time on data collection activity. The test suite must have the real-time console popping out the numbers and patterns on executions instantaneously. It should classify test cases based on scenarios, components, use cases, etc. These factors matter and add speed in test executions enabling swifter development and go to market.

Ensure test environment and data

The test environment and data is a central part of the testing strategy. The team should not wait for the data from production or other sources. Instead, the testing squad should commence on it as soon as the project is kicked off so that they can start testing the functionality with the test data mockups or stubs in the lower environment. Setting up the test data and the environment sometimes takes longer than anticipated. It requires the engagement of other teams - IT Operations, Cloudops, Information Security, Firewall, Network Security, etc. who evaluates the data needs and ensures its compliance with integrity, regulatory, and security attributes. Therefore, these steps and time should account for in the project plan.

Test data generation must be done before the test execution phase; else, it will affect the overall testing schedule. There are numerous ways test data can be generated from manual to copying from production to auto-generating it through a tool. The team should evaluate all options and select the best possible way to meet their purpose. Test cases and data should be maintained and updated regularly as per the changes in the product. We generally miss out on keeping it renovated and relevant. It should be altered or added if there is new functionality or deprecation of an old one. The test management tool should always reflect the latest state of the test cases in congruence with the product. The smoke and regression suites must be up to date with the pertinent test cases that are added new for any functionality or a critical flow. These upfront measures prevent the loss of team efforts to perform a mundane clean-up later on.

Empower your testers

As an engineering manager, you should provide absolute freedom to your testers. Empower and support them to break the code and uncover bugs as many as they can. It is often noticed that the engineering manager would try to influence on limiting the defects and urging testers to provide sign-off, even with open critical issues in the software. This approach will prove catastrophic once the customers start witnessing those issues, resulting in substandard product experience. You should encourage your testing team to do a thorough and systematic job in ensuring good quality before it is shipped to the customers. They should own the ultimate signing authority to provide a go / no-go decision on the product release in the market. The confidence in the complete product quality should depend on the passing rate, percentage of the test cases, and the sustenance of its stability. You need to safeguard your testers not to get influenced or compelled by anyone.

Have the right and optimal product certification policy

Agile, DevOps, and lean methodologies are being embraced by the product organizations to speed up their program development. However, there are difficulties in identifying the right levels and the technique for product quality. There are disputes in determining the factors impacting the software quality and the associated plan/metrics to measure them on an on-going basis. Different products based on their usage, type, and hosting environment will have different elements that play a significant role in its quality.

Software excellence is a default expectation by an end-user and the customer using the product. They do not care if the issue is in the functional or non-functional requirements. For them, it does not matter if the problem is in performance or security. What matters to them is the wholesome experience that they have while using the product, the ease with which they can get glued to it, and have a seamless user experience. With that in mind, the testing leaders in the team should come up with the precise low-level strategy to test and provide sign-off on the product deliverables. It is analogous to the design phase of the development. The product objective, intended features, customer touchpoints, and use cases should be articulated and laid out upfront. Then, the testing strategy must be devised per the engineering and product team.

Make use of analytics to monitor defects and customer sentiments

If the product is already in use by the customers, then the obvious step is to find pain points for them that they are witnessing during the product usage. Customers will vent out their aggravations about the product on social media and various online platforms. So, it becomes the first place for an engineering manager to probe and come up with an out-of-box method to find out the troubled components and modules in the product. Traditional ways to gather the voluminous data and insights from it will be cumbersome. It will be a time-consuming and worthless effort. Instead, you should leverage analytical techniques to do a defect and sentiment analysis using some of the proven classification models.

Sentiment is a prominent type of information conveyed in human language, which should be technically leveraged. Customer sentiment, being key to any product and software success, should be regularly measured, and suitable steps need should be taken frequently. In the IT product & services landscape, where the business depends more than 90% on the repeat customers, their sentiments and perception about the product and service becomes even more meaningful to the organization.

Legacy quality testing and assurance approach concentrated only on certifying business and functional requirements. There are support teams in service and product companies to track production defects and turn them around as per defined SLA (Service Level Agreement). But, is this sufficient enough in today's market to tackle customer issues? Certainly Not. Testing is confined to business or technical requirements but lacks customer's usage patterns, which induces a gap between engineering understanding and customer expectations. Also, the rapid change in the technology stack and application complexity is even posing more complexity to testing and quality assurance unit.

With the spotlight on customer defects, product research and development unit should transform their production defect management to a more intelligent and insightful division, with simultaneous mining of data, text, and customer sentiment analytics from various online platforms and channels. A surfeit of data and actionable insights can be excavated from production incidents and logs at a much faster pace.

For example, below are the step-by-step procedure to it using sentiment analysis technique,

1. **Determine high-frequency terms** – Identify terms in the incident subject and description with a higher rate of occurrence. These terms are potential problematic zones in the product impacted or the cause of the failure of other pieces.

2. **Find out association and strength of correlation between terms** – establishes a relationship between terms and reveals hidden affiliation indicating patterns or the causes of failures.

3. **Topic modeling** – This step unveils latent and hidden topics using the LDA (Linear Discriminant Analysis) classification

technique. It creates clusters of closely associated topics and terms with the occurrence frequency against a timeframe.

4. **Customer emotional valence and sentiment score** – This step charts out sentiment pattern and mood swings on the scale of negativity, curiosity, sadness, anger, positivity, etc. There are various libraries available to use as per the fitment of the model.

The data points from the above procedure derives the actionable comprehensions. You can program the steps to get timely information on the console or a dashboard. It identifies the mood pattern of your customers and the cause of it with pointers to troubling components in the product. It also gives you the duration and moments of spikes in sentiment swings. With this, you can knit your product usage trend by the customers over a while. It could be due to the launch of a new feature or a promotional campaign or the spur due to festive and holiday seasons.

It enables support functions to have a preemptive maintenance mechanism in place, allowing them to prioritize and fix issues in co-related areas as well. Risk management is more profound by prioritizing critical regions in the software, test and repair them upfront to avoid cropping up of any malfunctions or unknown effects. The engineering unit should strategize some more testing and regression in these existing components and the ancillary parts related to it, before they plan to release the next version. Broadly, it not only improves the product class but also enhances customer experience and company brand.

Thorough impact assessment in engineering DNA

Impact assessment is a critical aspect in software engineering, neglected or not done with due diligence by the teams, eventually leaking bugs in the product. You can scrutinize the impact of component failure if you are well-versed with the functional, code, and data flow. In simple terms, impact analysis is done to identify the area of code change and the linked functionality that is impacted or may be affected by that code change. Bugs are expensive if not caught at the budding state of the product. Leaked ones will surface in production, but causing damage to the product name in the market.

The engineering slipup is either the impact evaluation is completely missed or done if a defect filed. Impact evaluation is not a one-time exercise; instead, it is an on-going one. It must be performed at all levels of development. The feature development in the product never stops; you keep on building and releasing versions of it. Therefore, the impact analysis becomes an implicit necessity. A comprehensive effect study would also help the testing team to concentrate on those affected elements instead of testing the entire product set. It narrows to targeted functional and regression validation, cutting down the testing span and thrusting deployments.

Impact study of the change should be documented, preferably in the JIRA story itself. It becomes a good reference point for all the engineers not only at that point but also for future reference. The study should cover all possible outcomes of the change and the affected modules due to it. It should pinpoint all code files, documents, models, objects, tables, etc. that require modification due to the change. It should also contain a list of all tasks, and its sequence must account for that modification. More the information, it becomes much easier for developers and testers to ensure the right coverage of their respective testing.

The impact research should consist of the NFRs that may get potentially influenced. For example, a change in the flow of the functionality might blow NFRs usability and performance. It guarantees that the performance and user experience testing is carefully done without any undesirable impact on the customer. Usually, we miss out on NFRs, which are essential to any product success story. The performance tests should be compared with the benchmarks provided by product management. Finally, once the impact analysis is complete, the tester should identify all the test scenarios and cases applicable to the change. Constant communication between the developer and the tester is inevitable. The test cases should be reassessed by the product owner, primarily the customer use cases.

Follow change management and estimate efforts

Effort estimation post-impact assessment is a mandatory step. It feeds into a detailed planning with the right expectations setting with stakeholders and customers. Estimation will be done based on the complexity of the change. Teams can use any various estimation techniques, but the intent is to have the time, and the cost accounted for due to the change. This exercise facilitates rank-ordering if there are multiple change requests with a similar urgency from the stakeholders and business. Cost and time play a crucial role in determining the priority of the change. The active program plan should be recalibrated if there is an impact to it due to the new change request. Relevant transmission of information and message should happen to stakeholders pertinent to the effort and plan.

The matured organization has a predefined change request and impact assessment templates that capture the important points. It is archived in the knowledge repository once the change is deployed in production. It not only helps the team to have process standardization but also aligns the stakeholders and CCB (Change Control Board) that act as a gate approvers to provide go/no-go ahead to every production release.

Automate optimally

Urgency should be to automate testing as it saves the cost and time of the engineering function. It pushes to deliver faster and deploy quicker in production. It removes the reliance on individuals, and it can run continuously for hours together without being fretted of the shift rosters and individual's availability. Within the automation charter, the preference should be on the frequent-running test cases. The obvious candidates for automation are smoke, regression, performance, load, and newly-added features that will run more often - a higher rate of testing occurrence, more precedence for it to be automated. The aim should never be to automate anything and everything. Reaching 100% automation milestone does not necessarily mean that the coverage is 100%. It can be manipulated easily in the test case management system. Instead, the guiding principle should be to have optimal automation to have maximum coverage. The critical paths of the product where there is no human intervention required, should be prime flows for automation.

Stagger and throttle your releases

Explore the option of releasing alpha and beta versions of your product to the customers. You can also publish your product or the new functionality in a throttled manner, which means that you open the new functionality in production only to a selected user base. This user base is the one who volunteer to test your product & features and provide you immediate feedback. They will also share their point of view. In this way, you get the pulse of your customer perception about the product/feature and can accordingly take a call on whether to release it to everyone or roll it back.

It is a comprehensive validation policy imbibed by companies to seek early and quick customer opinion, and stabilize it by resolving reported issues. It works well in case of any greenfield product development where the product or the engineering team has no historical data on the usage & acceptance of the product, when there is uncertainty on customer's usage and adoption. The product team can also release features in a phased manner rather than putting it all out in one shot.

This mechanism also helps the engineering team to test the waters before diving entirely into it. For example, if they intend to release a performance breakthrough in their product, they can check it with the release to a shortlisted customer base, instead of broadcasting it to everyone.

Strive for excellence and success will be there inevitably

Chapter 9

Don't deal with metrics, lead with it

A metric is something that can be quantified and calculated. In computer programming, the metric is a measurement of a software characteristic. The metrics add value in product software development in many ways, including evaluating work items, development headway, productivity, product performance, quality, etc.

Within the software engineering course, numerous parameters can be measured and tracked. Is it required? The answer is NO.

The system of measurement you opt should apply to your software development voyage and add value to your business, by being effortlessly measurable, interpretable and actionable. The parameters should be readily obtainable, preferably automated to collate, examine and report. The process must have the least manual intervention to avoid efforts from anyone in the team.

Usually, the metrics collection and tracking it is a humdrum task for the team, and nobody willingly volunteers for it. It is desirable if the pre-configured systems spit out the data points, numbers, and associated patterns. Instantaneous accessibility of the metrics to comprehend and derive insights from it, is the icing on the cake for everyone.

Metric identification and tracking should drive the project unit towards its goals. The following are three essential objectives for any software development program/initiative.

- *Augment the **quality** of the product for better customer experience and retention.*
- *Improve the **efficiency** of the product development process for faster go-to-market.*
- *Increase **profitability** by regulating the project in terms of cost and schedule.*

Organizations experienced and established in their processes are embracing analytics and data science field to mine a glut of data to make rapid and speedier decisions.

There are broadly two levels for the need and consumption of the measured parameters. The metric-type is then mapped to the respective level.

First level – The engineering team

The vital indicators to track team productivity, feature development progress, defects, etc. are relevant for the engineering team to plan and prioritize their daily sprint work. These metrics are more useful and beneficial when the teammates are geographically distributed. The concept of a dispersed team is turning into a reality. Further, these indicators get classified into three frames of a 3P framework.

Product metrics

These indicators evaluate the state of the product, chiefly related to the in-making features, quality, and readiness of the product. Requirement traceability, risk assessment & mitigation, issue tracking, and defects are some of the metrics that need to be captured and monitored during the development course. The ability of the team to control quality, in terms of incoming vs. outgoing defects, is also assessed. Defect convergence and severity chart proves insightful to understand the quality level of the product.

The risk register is a journal where proactive risk assessment and mitigation steps are recorded, and deliberated. The project manager will continually keep an eye on these risks to take corrective and preventive actions accordingly. Risks and issues beyond the project team's control should be emphasized to the stakeholders at the appropriate time.

Code-specific metrics like coverage, cyclomatic complexity, code smells, commenting patterns, etc. should be monitored in real-time by developers and technical leads to ensure its conformance to coding standards and best practices. It also indicates, if teammates adhered to code reviews and secure-coding practices. Third-party licensing risks or any IP non-compliance should also be examined using open source security tools. There are tools available in the market that help in measuring these metrics in real-time, at the time of code checking-in the repository.

The metrics should also cover factors such as rework in product development, deployment - success versus rollbacks. It provides useful information on the frequency of its occurrence, and the meticulous root cause analysis can aid in correcting the blockades and fix the problem.

Process metrics

The purpose of tracking process metrics is to enhance the procedures and ways; the team follows during the product development trip. The fundamental thumb rule for these metrics is the process must be simplified to ease the adoption by the engineering group. It evaluates the engineering efficiency, the rate at of feature completion and verification of the features post its implementation. It also examines the adherence of developed functionality with its acceptance criteria.

It scrutinizes the process that is in place for quality control and if they need any improvements - defect resolution time, defect triaging mechanism, root cause analysis, and deployment protocol. These checkpoints facilitate to retrospect the process effectiveness, and the steps team follows to achieve the desired engineering goals.

Productivity metrics

Productivity metrics capture the characteristics of the team and their execution form. It provides evidence on their capacity, velocity, productivity, resource loading, cost incurred on the team, and product. These are critical metrics to determine the profitability of the software that you are building. It identifies the velocity and productivity of the team to take suitable measures to enhance it for faster and quality delivery. It also feeds in planning the next sprint and successive assignment of tasks more realistically and with more certainty.

Second level – The stakeholders, executive and senior management

The leadership and executive management are interested in the program at a high level. Their availability and attention is limited when it comes to learning every minor detail of the program. They usually are multi-tasking on other urgent priorities when you are presenting a program report to them. Therefore, the indicators should be simple to comprehend to make quick conclusions.

At a high level, they are interested mainly in three parameters - schedule, quality, and cost. The executives want to know if the program is on course or not. They want to know if the project is doing fine on budget. Is there a probable cost overrun or under control? The quality of the product is always a matter of worry for the management as it impacts the customers directly. Quality must be ranked on the top as it determines the product usage by customers and have implications on the company's revenue and profitability.

Post categorizing the metrics that will be relevant for your software product, teams, and executive management; the next essential step is to present it. You may be capturing the finest data and metrics, almost real-time. Still, it fails to have an impact on the recipients unless produced skillfully with appropriate visuals and graphs.

Data visualization is the next significant phenomenon today across all domains and businesses. It is transforming the way data is consumed in today's era. Infographics, graphs, data charts, moving images, etc. are enabling us to view and comprehend data not only from different angles but also quickly. I have always ensured that the mechanism of data collection and reporting is coherent and self-explanatory in my program reports. The basic rule to follow is that it should never be complicated and overhead for my team and stakeholders.

I love to utilize the dashboard feature, which practically all leading software lifecycle management tools provide nowadays. There are impressive reporting consoles that can be designed using Microsoft Project Planner, JIRA, and Confluence. These information consoles display the metrics pertinent to my program and consumed by my team and the executives. There are widgets and graphical tiles embedded in the dashboard and placed in such a way that a continual data story is knit with the right interpretation in the end.

There are various widgets for different information flashes. The relevant query is programmed to fetch the required data and then plugged in the widget. These widgets can be configured to refresh automatically at a defined interval. Below are a few examples of the widgets and the data point to be calibrated to flash corresponding numbers and trends. Each combination will provide you distinct insight that can be interpreted in many angles.

- Velocity of scrum team
- Defects as per priority
- Defects – Priority vs. Status
- Defects – As per components
- Created vs. Resolved defects
- Defect Ageing
- Heat Map

- Sprint Health Bar
- Sprint Burndown
- Sprint task list
- Features/Epics for a release
- % Completion statistics at epic/feature level
- Epics, stories and tasks vs. Status view
- Vital Parameters like automation coverage, code coverage

These data flashing consoles will only spit out numbers and some graphs, but they do not make any sense unless these numbers and trends have actionable derivation. It is the responsibility of the engineering and the project manager to keep reviewing these numbers and have an in-depth grip of the trends and patterns it shows. The underline message from these numbers must be translated to immediate curative measures for the benefit of the program. The metrics can either confuse you entirely with no meaning or can ultimately put you in the front seat, leading to a successful completion of the program with a better command on it.

Velocity

Velocity is a metric that shows the amount of work an agile team can complete within two or three weeks of sprint. It is primarily used to plan the capacity of the team based on the pace at which they complete the stories. It can be accumulated, and the overall project completion timeline can be forecasted. Typically, the velocity of a development team is constant at the initial stages, during the forming and norming phase. It increases during the later stages when they are in performing mode, before steadying as a plateau in the end. A careful assessment of the teams' historical trend on velocity will provide a sense of their consistency and predictability, ultimately feeding in the estimation and planning of the future sprint work.

Burndowns

A burndown graph is a visual representation of remaining work versus time. Burndown charts get populated with the data based on the work done by the engineers, at the same time logged in the system as well. It keeps a watch if the completed assignment is in line with its estimates. It is applied to predict if the work taken in the sprint will finish on time or spill. The initial trends exhibited by the burndown can use to do a course correction and remove impediments, if any, by the scrum master or the project manager. Burndowns are predominant in both agile and waterfall software development methodologies. The burndown charts apply to any project containing measurable improvement over effort and time.

Defects

A bug can disguise itself as a feature, if you do not have an eye on them. Scrutinizing and tracing bugs throughout the development voyage is an utmost need.

There are two essential viewpoints for showing defect metrics. One is to indicate the number of open defects as per the severity, and the other one is to reveal the trend of incoming versus resolved defects. Any software, if it has, the high number of blockers and critical bugs, stands a threat to its production rollout, if not contained promptly. Likewise, if the incoming and resolving defect trend is not converging, then it is a sign of worry as it poses a danger to the complete timeline and release. The defect should be tagged and labeled each time with the component/feature related to it. Discipline in enriching the defect with all the required details and labels allows the team to locate the most vulnerable and defective components in the product. Basis this, the team can plan additional testing and regression on those components, before releasing the next product version.

Correlation between quality, cost and schedule

It is critical to depict the correlation and trend between the quality, cost, and schedule of the project, especially to the executives. The relationship is directly proportional to each other. For example, if the schedule of the project is getting delayed, then the cost will also increase. Similarly, if the quality of the project is not under control, and there is a laundry list of defects to fix, it will again impact the cost and timelines of the project, increasing it further. My senior leadership and stakeholders have appreciated the concentric circular matrix as they acquire the view and correlation pattern immediately. It also shows how the project is transpiring and points to the quandaries for the program on the whole.

The parameters concerning product performance and impact to the customers must be traced. The engineering function should not cease its program post product deployment. They should be cognizant about how the customers are using and considering their product and work.

Metrics for customer satisfaction, product returns or recalls, reduction in service requests, customer churn rate must be chased to see the effect of the release. It also provides essential reasons for the team to retrospect if the underlying software engineering process and improvements have made any desired impact on the customers and sales.

Metrics should work for you and not the other way round.

Chapter 10

Foster decision-making and ownership

Ownership is to take charge of something and drive it to closure. Ownership cannot be accepted for just a phase or a stage at a person's will. It's about taking the end-to-end initiative to complete a particular job with the accountability of the result as well, more to bring out the desired and positive outcome. Taking ownership of your work, may sound simple, but is not easy for everyone. It brings in added responsibility, pressure, and obligation towards the team and the company in terms of results. While, in principle, it means the identical at all levels, the expectation from the role, involvement, and the result will be different.

Ownership for a developer is to code a module and functionality from the end-to-end use case viewpoint. If there are multiple modules where there is a handshake required between them, then he/she should own it to get those changes done in those modules by other teams, integrate and test it. The accountability should be entirely on the developer to interact and work in congruence with other colleagues and implement the customer use case. The developer cannot choose to take the ownership only for his element because that partially baked element is not going to fulfill the product functionality.

183

The general attitude observed in the developer is to code his own story without being informed about the progress on the dependent piece. There is no pairing with other teams. Likewise, a tester cannot just test the half-baked functionality and mark it as complete. The code examiner should wear a customer's hat all the time and check the functionality from origin to end. The engineer should always have the customer glasses on while developing and testing any product feature. The user experience will turn terrible if the serviceability, performance, and ease of the function is not deemed. This limited thinking will not only impede an individual's growth but also hinder the team's course as well.

Correspondingly, for an engineering manager/leader, the ownership is to deliver products and support it in production. He cannot do this alone; instead, he will have to constitute teams and build a product manufacturing and assisting factory. He may have several groups under him, but the definitive accountability on the delivery and its results lies with the manager. It's the responsibility on him to build the product within the budget and schedule.

Backing your teams, making suitable product choices, attending customer's problems with urgency are equally must for an engineering leader in demonstrating how ownership and decisions are taken up. Individuals with sheer intellect are great in individual contribution roles, but they face serious challenges when it comes to building and leading teams.

You should be very careful while taking or assigning ownership of a task. There is a thin line between taking ownership and start owning other's job. You will always find a few people around who will not hold responsibility for their work. They will be least worried about its completion on time, and callous about its implications. In the end, that incomplete work will be pushed on the person's shoulder, who is a sincere and dedicated professional. Now, he has to complete not only his own task but also the one given to that careless fellow. This transfer of work and responsibility should never happen.

Management should classify such non-productive individuals and provide them critical feedback. Stern action should be taken if they fail to mend their working style and commitment. The right message should cascade across the unit. Otherwise, it is not healthy for the team and will drag down the performance and morale of the high-performing players. The leaders should not even think twice to get rid of such employees from the company who are not meeting the work expectations on purpose.

On decision-making, it is projected that an average adult makes around 35,000 remotely conscious decisions every day. Every decision we make has an outcome. Decision making is relatively easy and straightforward when there are clarity and simplicity. However, it becomes tough when there are uncertainty and complexity—software development in a VUCA world. Also, on top of that, the technology is changing at a mind-boggling pace. Plus, the information is bombarded in abundance, making it unfeasible to soak up everything.

Software product development is a relentless problem-solving workout, with uncertainty and complexity entrenched in the entire process. The decision making is not plain and forthright as it has implications on the software, cost, and the customers. In such conditions, we humans tend to use alternate decision-making techniques. We tend to either avoid/deflect or delegate the decision making to someone else who has more knowledge and command on the subject. In that bid, we also conveniently pass the ownership to the other person. This delegation is wrong.

You must obtain the data points and information from an expert or a group required for decision-making. You may also choose to appoint someone to further research on the matter, but eventually, the ownership lies with you. It is unfair to pass on the ownership to others when it is supposed to be with you.

For example, as an engineering manager, you can brainstorm and ask for options for a technical implementation from your team, but finally, you need to decide on one plan. The result of that option is something you should own as a team representative. You may choose to defer the decision-making until you have the required information, and that is all right. A delayed decision is fine if it is a well-informed one. In the case of multiple teams and disciplines, it becomes practically tricky for one person to make all decisions. It creates dependency and delays, overwhelming one person. In such scenarios, you should decentralize the decision-making to a few reliable colleagues who have earned credibility from their hard work, persistence, and an impressive track record. Collectively, you still own up all the individual decisions and the respective consequences.

The peculiarity of a good decision-maker is to stay calm, composed, level-headed, investing the energy into the root cause of the problem.

With thorough analysis, they think it through from all possible angles, its impact, risk, and endings. At times, a decision may not benefit everyone immediately, but it should favor from a long term perspective. It is complicated for any engineering leader to lay off a team member from the company. It is a tough decision to make, but such decisions are unavoidable when an individual is a misfit for the team and is unable to meet the expectations of the group. Such folks, if they continue in the organization, will progressively impact the productivity of the entire unit, ultimately risking the project as a whole.

Impulsive decision making may not give you the desired results always as that's the decision you have taken in haste, without devoting effort to comprehend it. Such choices may look fine in the short term but are always risky from a long-term point of view. Therefore, you should desist from taking any irresponsible selection.

Companies are taking up analytics and machine learning techniques to make better and informed decisions. Business analytics is enabling senior executives and management with insights on market, competition, and alternative products. Companies are mining the volumes of data that they have and are using it for making strategic and tactical decisions. With data and trends, the decision can be straight forward while it will be a chaos; in the absence of it.

Data is the new oil, and companies are moving more and more towards digitization to extract information and pump that in their analytical prescriptive and predictive models to identify the trends near real-time. It helps them to make quick judgments and course-correct if they see any alarms in it. For example, a system-generated alert on the reduction of paper roll below a threshold value, in the receipt printer of an ATM is picked up by the central monitoring server. The server then flashes the details of that ATM on an information radiator in the command room, indicating the receipt printer will be out of paper in the next two days. The alert is routed to the closest available ATM technician of that specific vendor to refill the paper roll in that ATM within the next four hours. This entire process of detecting a probable anomaly and dispatching actionable alert to the vendor is entirely handled by systems, allowing predictive maintenance. The systems themselves discovered the issue, decided on selecting the vendor for the warning to be dispatched without human intervention or any manual process.

It's the onus of the engineering leader to mentor his team members on how to make effective decisions from the customer and company standpoint. It's the most undervalued skill in the software engineering world. Engineering leaders should have the knack to identify team members who could be groomed into future leaders and decision-makers. They must tie every choice they make, with the business in monetary value. That will avoid hasty rulings that may prove detrimental to the company.

A specific technical hitch for a developer might be new for him but not new for others. That same problem might have already been solved, and hence the developer should not try to reinvent the solution but to see if one of the existing solutions fit and will solve the problem. Decision making should be smart as well, wherever required. Freshers or new software engineers should learn when to consult their peers, seniors, or technical leads when they face any problem. They must do the groundwork and study to understand the problem better before they quest for a solution.

A critical defect discovered on the day of the production release, and now the release manager must decide whether to let it go or roll back the version. It is a tough call to make, and he can make a compelling choice if he knows the impact of that defect to its customers. If the error is breaking only one secluded functionality, then the product can still be released with that as a known defect, which the team can fix in war footing mode. But if it is a fault in the core piece, then holding off the release is a better decision.

Product development shops are nowadays doing the Canary or Blue-Green deployments wherein the product or functionality is released only to the subset of users in a throttled manner. This way, it is not rolled out to everyone at one go, lowering the risk of releasing bugs and defects to the customers. Such production roll-out tactic must be evaluated, based on the nature of the product and its customers, to minimize risk induction.

Study shows that we fall prey to our default mental shortcuts, cognitive biases, that influence our decisions. We need to get better at it, and it will come only through experience and more knowledge. Critical thinking with objective analysis and evaluation of a problem helps in making fewer errors in decision making.

Requirement gathering and prioritization is another essential aspect where decision making plays a vital role. The product management must make an unbiased call in shortlisting the features to build in the product. This process involves tradeoffs and adjustments between the product and engineering functions. Both teams must be confident that the outcome of the prioritization exercise should meet customer needs and delight them. For that, the product owner cannot make decisions solely on their gut feel. They need to do due diligence in terms of market research, both primary and secondary. They should survey customers and obtain inputs. Based on the study, they must validate their interpretation of the market demand from the analyst community like Gartner, Forrester, Nelson-Hall, IDC, etc. They should also deliberate on every feature and classify the revenue-generating ones and good-to-have ones. That makes it relatively straightforward for the engineering team to prioritize and plan accordingly. The more informed decision making done at the start, the less it becomes prone to errors at the later stage. In case of a rash and sub-optimal decision, it proves pricier later on.

Bug triaging process is another example that we deal very often in our software development lifecycle. The engineering, product, and customer service unit would contend and discuss on the bugs reported from production. The incident report is often incomplete with relevant data like occurrence time, impacted customers, and the user base. There are no logs and screen snapshots of the error attached in the incident report. The description in the bug report is incomplete and ambiguous.

Consequently, a lot of time is squandered on agreeing on the severity and impact of the bug. Imagine, if the needed data is available in the incident report, then the decision-making would have been more rational and faster. Analytics and machine learning mechanisms should be utilized to support the choice-making if all the evidence is present in the report. Classification modeling can classify the bugs in the right category systemically. Further on, prescriptive analytics can also be brought into the picture to suggest probable solutions on those bugs. The facilitator should set up a recurring connect with all participants from different units and ensure that the report contains all the information before it is picked up for triaging.

Decision making can be a step-by-step process. A systematic and logical approach will help in covering all the critical aspects and have more certainty on positive outcomes. This approach is principally based on information that is available before making the verdict. It also provides the stakeholders with the clarity and the basis on which the decision was made. It perpetually saves a lot of time in communicating, convincing, and aligning the stakeholders, post-verdict. There are three simple steps for effective decision making.

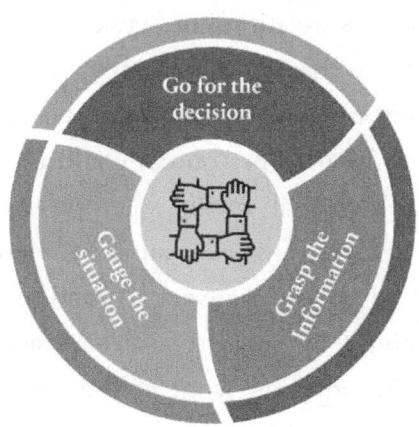

Step 1 – Grasp the information

First and foremost, is to gather the required information and data. You should make a list of all stakeholders and interested parties that will be impacted by the decision or should be made aware of the decision. Then comes the preferred result projected from the decision. It could be a strategic one - to improve profitability or improve customer experience. The result could also be a tactical one - to improve the quality and stability of the product.

Realizing the expected results is vital for the next set of information to determine and gather. Unless the expected result is known, you will not be able to collect the relevant data for it.

The subsequent ask is the data and the sources of that data. The data should be made available to you in the form that is easy to interpret and provides a pattern & relationship between it. You cannot have the unstructured data as that is not palatable and of no use. Logical levels of aggregations and abstraction should be done if the data is enormous and voluminous. The sources could be internal systems and external as well. Social media platforms, online feedback channels, internal tracking systems, advisory reports, primary & secondary research, and many more are all valid sources of the data. The data source should be genuine and have accurate data. You should also seek opinions from your colleagues, experts, or from someone who has spent more time handling similar situations in the past. You may also validate the pulse of your team/colleagues before the judgment. These moves avoid any cynical twist, or any unforeseen surprise post the verdict is pronounced.

Step 2 – Gauge the situation

The second step is to investigate and examine the situation/problem for which a decision needs to be made. There are multiple ways to analyze the problem and its root cause. Five Whys, Fishborne, etc. are some of the proven techniques used to deep dive and investigate the situation. You cannot make an effective decision unless you know the current situation and the problem that you intend to solve. The objective of this step is to identify and come up with a clear problem statement that can be understood by everyone.

You should abstain from solving all the problems simultaneously. Instead, you must concentrate on one at a time. Post your analysis; you should not only have the clasp on the condition but also be aware of the parties (customers, teams, stakeholders, vendors, etc.) that are part of it. You should also check if a similar situation had arisen earlier and the choice made at that time. It may not be an apple to apple comparison but will provide you leads in coming up with the right choice.

Step 3 – Go for the decision

Now that you have all the required information and analysis done list down all the alternatives for the decision. Evaluate each of these alternatives and choose the best fit one. You can never be a hundred percent confident about the consequence of the choice that you take. But you can opt for the one that is in the best interest of the customers, company, or the stakeholders, by settling the problem.

Once the option is selected, the next essential step is to document it and notify it to everyone.

Communiqué brings alignment and preparedness. You should be transparent with everyone on the choice that you made and share the reasons behind it. The stakeholders, impacted parties, and the teammates will appreciate and support your call if there is openness in the information. Sometimes, you may also need to over-communicate, considering the insecurity and vagueness in the situation. It provides assurance and positivity among the teammates. Decisions must always be recorded with the supporting data points and a list of impacted factions for future reference. The documented choices, in the past, can be referred anytime if a similar situation arises in the future. The scenarios may differ a bit, but the alternatives and the basis on which the choice made proves to be handy and useful.

The above three steps provide a framework for systematic, informed, and logical decision-making. The key is to stand by your decision and own the consequence, irrespective it was desired or otherwise. You should never blame anyone or pass on the liability, if your choice does not transform into preferred results.

You, as an engineering leader, must coach your team and provide them enough and more opportunities for making decisions at their levels and own them completely. You should assign one story/task to one team member, set the expectations, and support them so that they can hold it right from concept to deployment. Ownership brings in further commitment, resulting in watchful decision-making during the course. It is how you can nurture your teammates in making choices on smaller tasks at the start, earn confidence, and take possession of more substantial roles that have high stakes and visibility.

The core values of the company should have an ownership right on the top. The leadership should foster the culture through various means. Providing opportunities, trainings, mentorship programs, and, most importantly, support them even if they falter in their pursuit are some of the avenues for the leadership to have continual emphasis.

Customers love to work with collaborative leaders who do not just meet the requirements; instead, the leaders must partner with them, recognize, empathize with their situation, and provide the right solution to them. Clients also appreciate leaders who are direct and do not mince words simply to please them. They must highlight the problem upfront and have an honest dialogue with the customers. It can be done by individuals who are competent and confident in decision making, with owning it.

The best-rated workplaces around the world believe in you, empowers you to make choices and drive it with ownership. Change is unavoidable, and it is now a fundamental part of the software industry. Customer demands, market, and competition are on a transformational path. The rapid pace at which the change is happening creates more significant problems, which makes the leaders struggle to cope up with it. The leaders who cannot adapt to this new normal, in gauging, grasping the situation, and going for timely decisions will wane.

Leaders must capitalize on the change with courage and competence, shape and lead the path, as trailblazers.

About the book

Research has shown that 72% of new software products and services innovation fails to deliver on expectations. It implies 7 out of 10 products are outright rejected by the customers as soon as they are launched. Failure to understand customer needs and fixing a non-existent problem are the primary reasons for these products and services to fail.

The primary cause of the collapse could be a dearth of customer focus and rigor during the product development and engineering journey. There are various other internal dynamics within the company and the engineering unit for the downfall of the product. It could be distorted vision & goals, misaligned stakeholders, inadequate demarcation of roles and responsibilities, incoherent engineering processes, lack of discipline, compromising view towards quality, and incompetency in timely decision-making. It leads to wastage of everyone's time in unplanned, random tasks without any unified goal for the team, perpetually resulting in defective software product versions in the market, and substandard customer experience.

Cacophony to Symphony is a step by step guide to transform the software product development shop from chaos to order, from discord to harmony. It walks you through the proven techniques to build software in a much simplified and efficient manner by mitigating, maneuvering through the uncertainties and complexities of the software ecosystem.

The book plunges in the crucial facets of software engineering voyage, that are typically overlooked in a rush to create and deliver products faster. It serves a single point of reference for anyone who plans to venture in a start-up or set up a product development garage from scratch. It is also useful for the small and medium-sized product companies aspiring to shift gears and grow exponentially with better market relevance and sustenance. The book offers you with the fundamental blocks along with its right placement to build a seamless product manufacturing system through standardized processes, best practices with customer-centricity.

The engineering, project, program managers, and aspiring software management professionals will find this book as a ready reference for their encounters and queries pertaining to software development and program execution from concept to delivery.

Made in the USA
Monee, IL
07 July 2026